T0076143

EXCEL 2013/2016:
GET YOUR HANDS DIRTY

SAM AKRASI

Copyright © 2019 by Sam Akrasi. 769743
Library of Congress Control Number: 2018903587

ISBN: Softcover   978-1-5434-0751-8
        Hardcover   978-1-5434-0752-5
        EBook   978-1-5434-0750-1

All rights reserved. No part of this book may be reproduced
or transmitted in any form or by any means, electronic or
mechanical, including photocopying, recording, or by any
information storage and retrieval system, without permission
in writing from the copyright owner.

Print information available on the last page.

Rev. date: 04/18/2018

To order additional copies of this book, contact:
Xlibris
1-800-455-039
www.xlibris.com.au
Orders@Xlibris.com.au

Contents

1. Customizing the Excel User Interface 9

    1.1. Customizing the Quick Access toolbar (QAT) 9

        1.1.1 About the QAT 9

        1.1.2 Adding new commands to the Quick Access toolbar 9

        1.1.3 Other Quick Access toolbar actions 11

    1.2 Customizing the Ribbon 11

        1.2.1 How to customize the Ribbon 12

        1.2.1.1 Creating a new tab 12

        1.2.1.2 Creating a new group 13

        1.2.1.3 Adding command to a new group 13

        1.1.2 Resetting the Ribbon 13

2. Using Custom Number Formats 14

    2.1 About Number Formatting 14

        2.1.1 Formatting numbers by using the Ribbon 14

        2.1.3 Using the Format Cell dialog box to format numbers 15

    2.2 Creating a Custom Number Format 16

        2.2.1 Components of a number format string 16

        2.2.2 Custom number format codes 19

    2.3 Custom Number Format Examples 20

        2.3.1 Scaling values 20

        2.3.1.1 Displaying values in thousands 21

        2.3.1.2 Displaying values in millions 21

        2.3.2 Displaying leading zeros 22

        2.3.3 Specifying conditions 22

        2.3.4 Displaying fractions 22

        2.3.5 Formatting dates and times 22

        2.3.6 Displaying text with numbers 23

3. Using Data validation 24

    3.1 About Data Validation 24

    3.2 Specifying Validation Criteria 24

    3.3 Experimenting with the Validation Criteria 25

    3.4 Creating a Drop-Down List 25

3.5   Using Formulas for Data Validation Rules 25

3.6   Understanding Cell References 25

3.7   Data Validation Formula Examples 26

    3.7.1   Accepting text only 26

    3.7.2   Accepting larger value than the previous cell 26

    3.7.3   Accepting non-duplicate entries only 26

    3.7.5   Accepting dates by the day of the week 27

    3.7.7   Creating a dependent list 28

4.   Creating and Using Worksheet Outlines 30

   4.1   Creating an Outline 30

    4.1.1   Preparing the data 30

   4.2   Working with outlines 31

    4.2.1   Displaying levels 31

    4.2.2   Adding data to an outline 31

    4.2.3   Removing an outline 31

    4.2.4   Adjusting the outline symbols 31

    4.2.5   Hiding the outline symbols 32

5.   Linking and Consolidating Worksheets 33

   5.1   Creating External Reference Formulas 33

    5.1.1   Understanding link formula syntax 33

    5.1.2   Creating a link formula by pointing 33

    5.1.3   Pasting links 34

   5.2   Working with External Reference Formulas 34

    5.2.1   Opening a workbook with external reference formulas 35

    5.2.2   Changing the start-up prompt 36

    5.2.3   Updating links 36

    5.2.4   Changing the link source 36

    5.2.5   Severing link 36

   5.3   Consolidating Worksheets 37

    5.3.1   Consolidating worksheets by using formulas 37

    5.3.2   Consolidating worksheets by Using Paste Special 37

    5.3.3   Consolidating worksheets by using the Consolidate dialog box 38

    5.3.4   A workbook consolidation example 38

6.   Protecting Your Work 39

   6.1   Types of Protection 39

   6.2   Protecting a Worksheet 39

    6.2.1   Unlocking cells 39

    6.2.2   Sheet protection options 40

    6.2.3   Assigning user permissions 40

   6.3   Protecting a Workbook 41

    6.3.1   Requiring a password to open a workbook 41

6.3.2   Protecting a workbook's structure 42

6.4   VB Project Protection 43

6.5   Related Topics 43

6.5.1   Saving a worksheet as a PDF file 43

6.5.2   Marking a workbook final 44

6.6.3   Inspecting a workbook 44

7.   Making a Workbook Error Free 45

7.1   Finding and Correcting Formula Errors 45

7.1.1   Mismatched parentheses 45

7.1.2   Cells are filled with hash marks 45

7.1.3   Blanks are not blank 45

7.1.4   Formula returning an error 46

7.1.4.1   #DIV/0! Errors 46

7.1.4.2   #N/A errors 46

7.1.4.3   #Name? errors 46

7.1.4.4   #NULL! Errors 46

7.1.4.5   #NUM! errors 47

7.1.4.6   #REF! errors 47

7.1.4.7   #VALUE? Errors 47

7.1.5   Absolute/relative reference problems 47

7.1.6   Operator precedence problems 48

7.2   Using Excel Auditing Tools 48

7.2.1   Identifying cells of a particular type 48

7.2.2   Viewing formulas 48

7.2.3   Tracing cell relationships 49

7.2.3.1   Identifying precedence 49

7.2.3.2   Identifying dependents 50

7.2.4   Tracing errors values 50

7.2.5   Fixing circular reference errors 51

7.2.6   Using the background error-checking features 51

7.2.7   Using the Formula Evaluator 52

7.3   Using AutoCorrect 52

8.   Introducing Formulas and Functions 54

8.1   Understanding Formula Basics 54

8.1.1   Using operators in formulas 54

8.1.2   Understanding operator precedence in formulas 54

8.1.3   Using functions in formulas 55

8.1.3.1   Function arguments 55

8.2   Entering Formulas into Worksheet 59

8.2.1   Entering formulas manually 59

8.2.2   Entering formulas by pointing 59

      8.2.3   Pasting range names into formulas 59

      8.2.4   Tips for entering functions 60

   8.3   Using Cell References in Formulas 61

      8.3.1   Relative, absolute and mixed references 61

      8.3.2   Changing the Types of References 62

      8.3.3   Referencing cells outside the worksheet 62

      8.3.3.1   Cells in other worksheets 62

      8.3.3.2   Cells in other workbooks 62

   8.4   Using Formulas in Tables 63

      8.4.2   Using formulas within a table 64

      8.4.3   Referencing data in a table 65

      8.4.4   Specifying when formulas are calculated 65

   8.5   Using names for constants 65

   8.6   Using names for formulas 66

   8.7   Using range intersection 66

   8.8   Applying names to existing references 68

9.   Text Manipulating Functions 69

   9.1   Determining whether two strings are identical 69

   9.2   Joining two or more cells 69

   9.3 Displaying formatted values as text 69

   9.4 Displaying formatted currency values as text 70

   9.5 Removing excess spaces and nonprintable characters 70

   9.6 Counting characters in a string 70

   9.7 Changing the case of a text 70

   9.8 Extracting characters from a string 71

   9.9 Replacing text with other text 71

   9.10 Finding and searching within a string 71

   9.11 Searching and replacing within a string 72

10.   Working with Dates and Times 73

   10.1   How Excel Handles Dates and Times 73

      10.1.1   The time serial numbers 73

      10.1.2   Entering times... 73

   10.2   Working with Date-Related Worksheet Functions 73

      10.2.1   Displaying the current date 74

      10.2.2   Displaying any date 74

      10.2.3   Converting a nondate string to a date 74

      10.2.4   Calculating the number of days between two dates 75

      10.2.5   Calculating the number of workdays between two dates 75

      10.2.6   Offsetting a date using only workdays 75

      10.2.7   Determining the day of the week 76

      10.2.8   Determining a day's quarter 76

10.3 Working with Time-Related Worksheet Functions 76

    10.3.1 Displaying the current time 77

    10.3.2 Displaying any time 77

    10.3.3 Calculating the difference between two times 77

    10.3.4 Working with non-time-of-day values 77

11. Creating Formulas That Counts and Sum 78

    11.1 Counting and Summing Worksheet Cells 78

    11.2 Basic Counting Formulas 78

        11.2.1 Counting the total number of cells 79

        11.2.2 Counting blank cells 79

        11.2.3 Counting non-blank cells 79

        11.2.4 Counting numeric cells 79

        11.2.5 Counting text cells 79

        11.2.6 Counting non-text cells 80

        11.2.7 Counting logical values 80

    11.3 Advanced Counting Formulas 80

        11.3.1 Using the COUNTIF function 80

        11.3.2 Counting cells based on multiple criteria 81

        11.3.2.1 Using the "And" criteria 82

        11.3.2.2 Using the OR criteria 83

        11.3.2.3 Combining And and Or criteria 83

        11.3.2.4 Conditional Sums Using a Single Criterion 83

12. Getting to Know the LOOKUP Formulas 85

    12.1 Introducing Lookup Formulas 85

    12.3 Basic Lookup Formulas 86

        12.3.1 The VLOOKUP Function 86

        12.3.2 The HLOOKUP Function 87

        12.3.3 The LOOKUP function 87

        12.3.4 Combining the MATCH and INDEX functions 88

        12.4.1 Looking up an exact value 89

        12.4.2 Looking up a value from multiple lookup tables 90

13. Introducing Array Functions 91

    13.1 Understanding Array Formula 91

    13.2 Creating an Array Constant 93

    13.3 Naming Array Constants 94

    13.4 Working with Array Formulas 94

        13.4.1 Entering an array formula 94

        13.4.2 Selecting an array formula range 95

        13.4.3 Editing array formulas 95

        13.4.4 Expanding or contracting a multicell array formula 95

    13.5 Some Examples of Multicell Array Formulas 95

13.5.1	Counting characters in a range	96
13.5.2	Using functions with an array	96
13.5.3	Summing three smallest values in a range	96
13.5.4	Counting text cells in a range	97
13.5.6	More Examples of Array Formulas	97
13.5.7	Single-Cell Array Formulas	97
13.5.8	Summing a range that contains errors	97
10.3.4.1	Counting the number of error values in a range	98
13.5.6.3	Summing the N largest values in a range	99
13.5.6.4	Computing an average that excludes zeros	99
13.5.6.5	Determining whether a particular value appears in a range	100
13.5.6.6	Counting the number of differences in two ranges	101
13.5.6.7	Determining whether a range contains valid values	102

EXERCISE 1	103
EXERCISE 2	103
EXERCISE 3	105

14.	Analysing Data with Tables	106
14.1	Converting a Range to a Table	106
14.2	Basic Table Operations	107
14.3	Sorting a Table	107
14.3.1	Performing a More Complex Sort	107
14.3.2	Sorting a Table in Natural Order	108
14.3.3	Sorting on Part of a Field	108
14.4	Filtering Table Data	109
14.4.1	Using Filter Lists to Filter a Table	109
14.4.2	Using Complex Criteria to Filter a Table	110
14.4.2.1	Setting Up a Criteria Range	110
14.4.2.2	Filtering a Table with a Criteria Range	111
14.4.3	Entering Computed Criteria	112
14.4.4	Copying Filtered Data to a Different Range	113
14.5	Excel's Table Functions	113
14.5.1	About Table Functions	113
14.5.2	Table Functions that Don't Require a Criteria Range	113
15.5.3	Table Functions That Accept Multiple Criteria	115
14.5.4	Table Functions That Require a Criteria Range	115
	=DGET(Parts[#All], "Cost", Criteria)	116

15.	Using Excel's Business Modelling Tools	118
15.1	Using What-If Analysis	118
15.1.1	Setting Up a One-Input Data Table	118
15.1.2	Adding More Formulas to the Input Table	120

15.1.3   Setting Up a Two-Input Table 121

15.2   Working with Goal Seek 122

15.2.1   How Does Goal Seek Work? 122

15.2.2   Running Goal Seek.. 122

15.2.3   Optimizing Product Margin 124

15.3   Working with Scenarios 125

15.3.1   Setting Up Your Worksheet for Scenarios 125

15.3.2   Adding a Scenario 125

15.3.3   Displaying a Scenario 126

15.3.4   Editing a Scenario 127

15.3.5   Generating a Summary Report 127

15.3.6   Deleting a Scenario 129

EXCEL EXERCISES 130

EXERCISE 1: QUESTIONS 130

EXERCISES 1 ANSWERS 145

EXERCISE 2 QUESTIONS 154

EXERCISE 2: ANSWERS... 167

EXERCISE 3: QUESTIONS & ANSWERS.. 174

EXERCISE 4: QUESTIONS & ANSWERS.. 187

1. Customizing the Excel User Interface

The main user interface in Excel consists of:

- The Ribbon
- The Quick Access toolbar
- Right-click shortcut menus
- Dialog boxes
- Task panes
- Keyboard shortcuts.

This section of the course describes how to make changes to two user components: The Quick Access toolbar and the Ribbon.

1.1. Customizing the Quick Access toolbar (QAT)

The Quick Access toolbar is always visible regardless of which Ribbon tag is selected. You can put all your frequently used commands on the Quick Access toolbar:

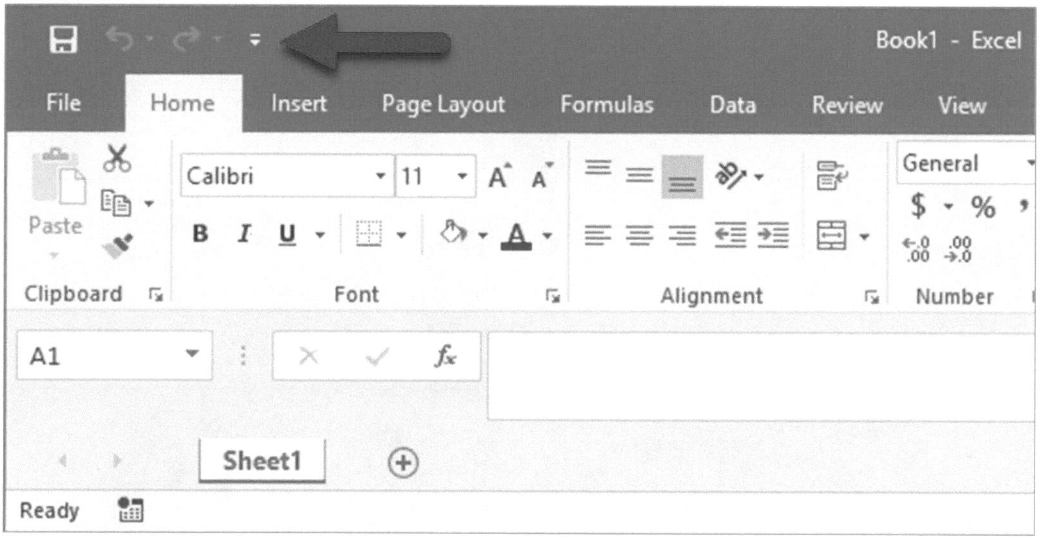

Figure 1.1

1.1.1 About the QAT

By default, the Quick Access toolbar is located on the left side of the Excel title bar, above the Ribbon (red arrowed in Figure 1.1 above). You can add commands to and remove commands from the Quick Access toolbar. You can also move the toolbar below the ribbon. To do so, right-click the toolbar and select **Show Quick Access Toolbar** below the Ribbon. To remove an icon from the Quick Access toolbar, just right-click the icon and from the context menu, select **Remove from Quick Access toolbar**. The positions of the icons can be rearranged through the Customize the Quick Access toolbar dialog box.

1.1.2 Adding new commands to the Quick Access toolbar

You can add a new command to the Quick Access toolbar in three ways:

1. Click the Quick Access toolbar drop-down control, located on the right side of the toolbar and select a command from the list that appears. See Figure 1.2a
2. Right-click any control on the Ribbon and choose Add to Quick Access Toolbar (Figure 1.2b)
3. Use the **Quick Access Toolbar** tab in **Excel Options** dialog box. A quick way to access this dialog box is to right-click any Ribbon control and choose Customize Quick Access Toolbar (Figure 1. 2c)

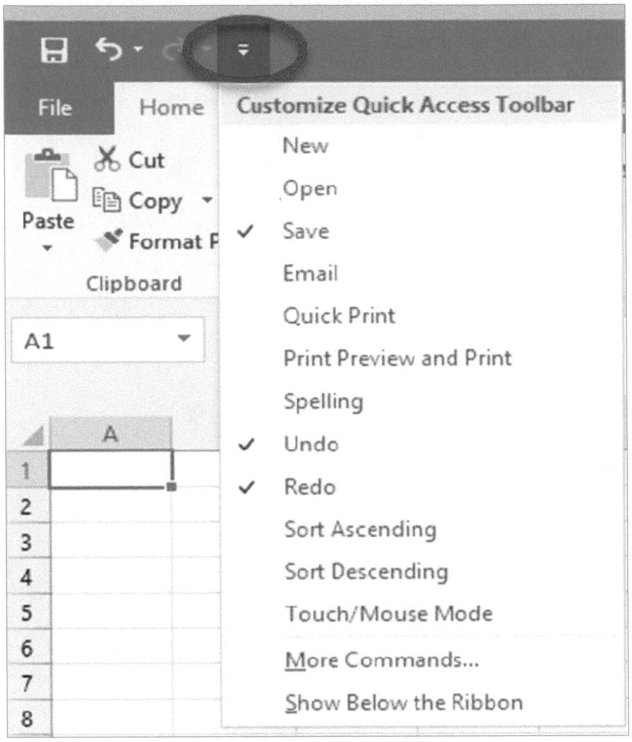

Figure 1.2a

Figure 1.2b

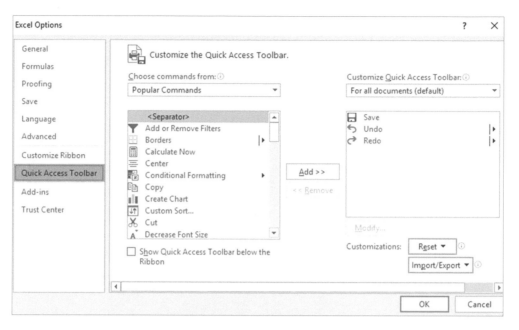

Figure 1.2c

Fig 1.2c shows the screen you get when you choose method 3 above. To add an item to the Quick Access toolbar, select it from the list on the left and then click **Add**. At the top of each list is an item called **<Separator>.** Adding this item to the Quick Access toolbar results in a vertical bar to help you group the commands. When you select Macro from the **Choose Command From** drop-down, Excel lists all available macros. If you add a macro to the Quick Access toolbar, you can click modify button to change the text and choose a different ion for the macro.

Ex1: Open the conditional sum.xlsx workbook. Create a macro for range A2:A11 (Macro1) to format the selected range as bold and change the row height to 24. Add the macro to the Quick Access toolbar and run it

1.1.3   Other Quick Access toolbar actions

- **Rearranging the Quick Access toolbar icons**: If you want to change the order of the Quick Access toolbar icons, you do so from the Quick Access Toolbar tab of the Excel Option dialog box. Select the command and then use the **Up** and **Down** arrow buttons on the right to move the icon.

- **Removing Quick Access toolbar icons**: To remove an icon from the Quick Access toolbar, right-click the icon and choose Remove from Quick Access Toolbar.

- **Resetting the Quick Access toolbar**: If you want to return the Quick Access toolbar to its default state, display the Quick Access Toolbar tab of the Excel Options dialog box and click **Reset** button. Then choose **Reset Only Quick Access Toolbar.**

1.2   Customizing the Ribbon

You can customize tabs on the Ribbon by:

- Adding new custom tabs

- Deleting custom tabs

- Changing the order of the tabs

- Changing a tab's name

- Hiding built-in tabs

You can customize groups on the Ribbon by:

- Adding new groups

- Adding commands to custom groups

- Removing commands from custom groups

- Removing groups from tabs

- Moving a group to a different tab

- Changing the order of the groups within a tab

- Changing the name of a group

1.2.1   How to customize the Ribbon

To customize the Ribbon, access the Customize Ribbon panel of the Excel Options dialog box as shown in Figure 1.3.

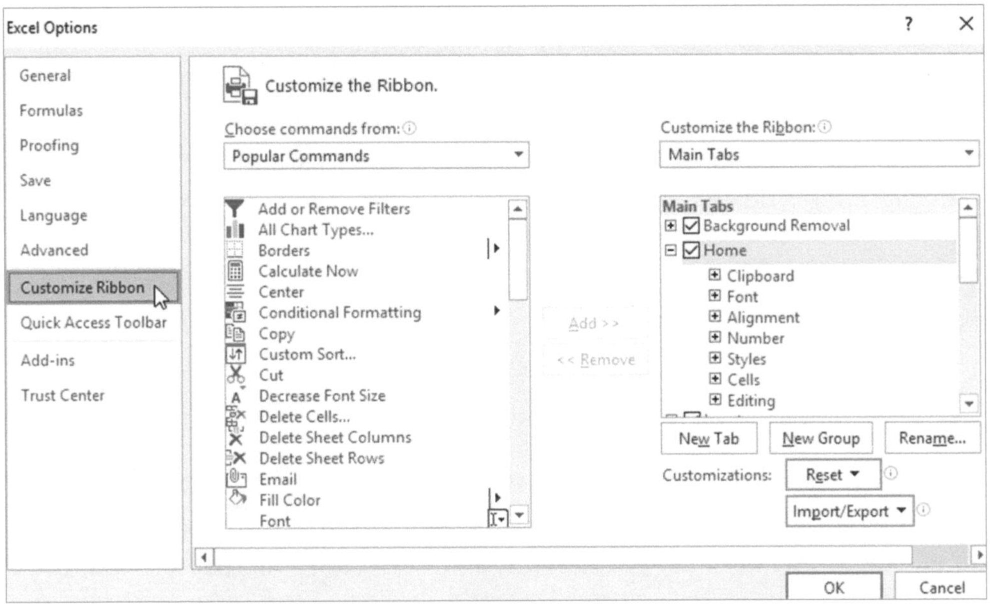

Figure 1.3

1.2.1.1   Creating a new tab

To create a new Ribbon tab, click the New Tab button (Figure 1.4). Excel creates a new tab called **New Tab (Custom)** and a new group called **New Group (Custom)** as a group for the new tab

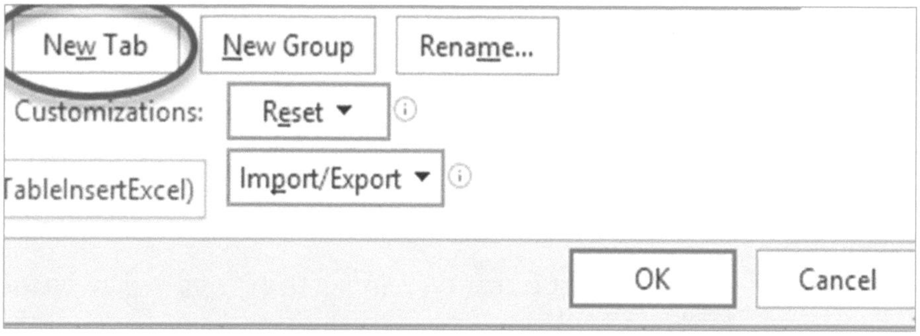

Figure 1.4

1.2.1.2   Creating a new group

To create a new group, select the tab that will hold the new group and click the New Group button. Excel creates a new group named **New Group (Custom)** which can be renamed.

1.2.1.3   Adding command to a new group

Commands must be placed in a new group. Here's the general procedure.

1. Use the **Choose Command From** drop-down list to display various groups of commands
2. Select the command in the list box on the left
3. Use the **Customize the Ribbon** drop-down list on the right to choose a group of tabs
4. In the list box on the right, select the tab and the group where you want to put the command.
5. Click the **Add** button to add the selected command from the left to the selected group on the right

1.1.2   Resetting the Ribbon

To reset all or part of the Ribbon to its default state, right-click any part of the ribbon and choose Customize the Ribbon from the shortcut menu. Excel displays the Customize Ribbon tab of the Excel Option dialog box. Click the Reset button to display two options: **Reset Only Selected Ribbon Tab** and **Reset All Customization**. If you select the latter, the Ribbon will be returned to its default state and you will also lose any Quick Access toolbar customization.

Exercise: Open the Ribbon Customization.xlsx workbook. Customize the Ribbon by creating a new tab. Rename the default group to Format Cells. Create a macro (use default name) that format the data as bold and sets the cell height to 25. Add the macro to the Format Cell group and run it. Reset the Ribbon.

2.   Using Custom Number Formats

Numbers in cells can be displayed in a variety of formats. In addition to the many built-in number formats, you can also create custom formats.

2.1   About Number Formatting

The key thing to notice about number format is that they are for display only. The actual number remains intact, and any formula that uses the formatted number uses the actual number.

> *Note: An exception to this rule occurs if you specify the Set Precision as Displayed option on the Advanced tab in the Excel Options dialog box. If that option is in effect, formulas use the values that are displayed in the cells as a result of a number format applied to the cells. In general, using this option is not a clever idea because it changes the underlying values in your worksheet.*

Excel automatically applies a built-in number format to cells based on the following criteria:

- If a number contains a slash (/), it may be converted to a date format or a fraction format

- If a number contains a hyphen (-), it may be converted to a date format

- If a number contains a colon (:), it may be converted to a date format or if followed by a space and the letter A or P (upper or lower), it may be converted to a time format

- If a number contains the letter E (upper or lower), it may be converted to scientific notation (e.g. 3.0E3). If the number doesn't fit into the column width, it may also be converted to this format.

2.1.1   Formatting numbers by using the Ribbon

The Number group contains some buttons that apply various formats to the active cell. In addition, the Number Format drop-down control provides 11 common number formats (Figure 1.5).

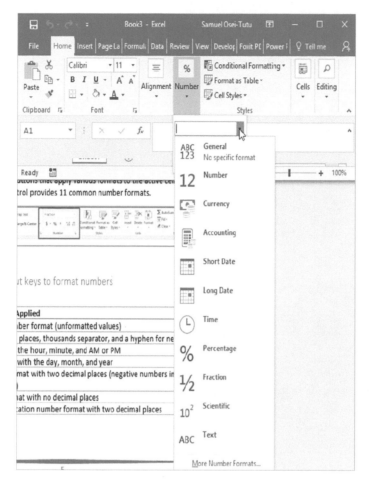

Figure 2.1

2.1.2 Using shortcut keys to format numbers

Table 2.1

Key Combination	Formatting Applied
Ctrl+Shift+~	General number format (unformatted values)
Ctrl+Shift+!	Two decimal places, thousands separator, and a hyphen for negative values
Ctrl+Shift+@	Format with the hour, minute, and AM or PM
Ctrl+Shift+#	Date format with the day, month, and year
Ctrl+Shift+$	Currency format with two decimal places (negative numbers in parentheses)
Ctrl+Shift+%	Percent format with no decimal places
Ctrl+Shift+^	Scientific notation number format with two decimal places

2.1.3 Using the Format Cell dialog box to format numbers

To access the Format Cell dialog box, you can use any of the following:

- Click the dialog box launcher at the bottom right of the Home Number group
- Choose **Home ⇒ Number ⇒ Number Format More Number Format**
- Press **Ctrl + 1**

Custom number formats can be used to format any cell in the workbook. Figure 2.2 shows the **Custom** category in the Number tab of the Format Cells dialog box.

```
Format Cells                                        ?    ✕

 Number   Alignment   Font   Border   Fill   Protection

 Category:
 ┌─────────────────┐   Sample
 │ General       ∧ │
 │ Number          │
 │ Currency        │   Type:
 │ Accounting      │   ┌──────────────────────────────────┐
 │ Date            │   │ General                           │
 │ Time            │   ├──────────────────────────────────┤
 │ Percentage      │   │ General                        ∧ │
 │ Fraction        │   │ 0                                │
 │ Scientific      │   │ 0.00                             │
 │ Text            │   │ #,##0                            │
 │ Special         │   │ #,##0.00                         │
 │ Custom          │   │ #,##0;-#,##0                     │
 │               ⌖ │   │ #,##0;[Red]-#,##0                │
 │                 │   │ #,##0.00;-#,##0.00               │
 │               ∨ │   │ #,##0.00;[Red]-#,##0.00          │
 └─────────────────┘   │ $#,##0;-$#,##0                   │
                       │ $#,##0;[Red]-$#,##0            ∨ │
                       └──────────────────────────────────┘
                                                   ┌────────┐
                                                   │ Delete │
                                                   └────────┘
 Type the number format code, using one of the existing codes as a starting point.


                                          ┌──────┐   ┌────────┐
                                          │  OK  │   │ Cancel │
                                          └──────┘   └────────┘
```

Figure 2.2

A custom number format consists of a format string made up of four-part codes separated by semicolons. The following is a simple number format code:

0.000

The code consists of placeholders and a decimal point; it tells Excel to display the value with three digits to the right of the decimal point.

2.2.1   Components of a number format string

A custom number format can have up to four sections which enable you to specify different format codes for positive numbers, negative numbers, zero values, and text. These codes must be separated by semicolons. The codes are arranged in the following order:

Positive format; Negative format; Zero format; Text format

You don't have to use all four sections. Table 2.2 below explains how Excel applies these codes to format cells:

Table 2.2

Section	1st Code	2nd Code	3rd Code	4th Code
1 only	Pos, Neg, Zero	N/A	N/A	N/A
1 & 2 only	Pos, Zero	Neg	N/A	N/A
1, 2 & 3 only	Pos	Neg	Zero	N/A
1, 2, 3, & 4	Pos	Neg	Zero	Text

Table 2.3

	Custom Format	Cell Entry	How it Appears
Using Text	#,##0 "US Dollars" "Answer: " General "The Amount is "#,##0" Dollars"	1500 1500 1500	1,500 US Dollars Answer: 1500 The amount is 1,500 Dollars
Scaling Large Numbers	#,##0, #,##0, #,##0,	123456789 12345678912 1234	123,456 12,345679 1
Data Validation	0.00;"No negative values!" 0.00;"No negative values!" 0.00;"No negative values!"	123 -123 0	123 No negative values 0
Zero with Dashes	#,##_);(#,##0);-0-_) #,##_);(#,##0);-0-_) #,##_);(#,##0);-0-_)	0 12.2 -12	0 12 (12)
Telephone Number	(###) ###-### ###"/"###-####	8005551212 8005551212	(800) 555-1212 800/555-1212
Social Security #	###-##-#### "SSN" ###-##-####	421897322 421897322	421-89-7322 SSN 421-89-7322
Date Formats	mmmm-yyyy mmmm d, yyyy mmmm d, yyyy (dddd) "It's" (dddd)	27/11/2017 27/11/2017 27/11/2017 27/11/2017	November-2017 November 27, 2017 Monday It's Monday

	Custom Format	Cell Entry	How it Appears
Different colours and formatting	[Red] [<1]0.0%;[Blue] [>=1] #,##0;General Red] [<1]0.0%;[Blue] [>=1] #,##0;General Red] [<1]0.0%;[Blue] [>=1] #,##0;General [Green]General; [Red]General; [Black] General;[Blue]General [Green]General; [Red]General; [Black] General;[Blue]General [Green]General; [Red]General; [Black] General;[Blue]General [Green]General; [Red]General; [Black] General;[Blue]General General;General;General;[Red]General General;General;General;[Red]General	1 -1 45 32 -32 0 text Only text is red 234	1 -100.00% 45 52 32 0 text Only text is red 234
Descriptive	"Positive"; "Negative";"Zero";"Text" "Positive"; "Negative";"Zero";"Text" "Positive"; "Negative";"Zero";"Text" "Positive"; "Negative";"Zero";"Tex	12 -32 0 Hello	Positive Negative Zero Text
Conditional	[>100]#,000;;; [>100]#,000;;; [>100]#,000;;; [>100]#,000;;; [<10]"Too low";[>10]"Too high";"Just right" [<10]"Too low";[>10]"Too high";"Just right" [<10]"Too low";[>10]"Too high";"Just right"	99 102 -54 Hello 5 12 10	102 Too low Too high Just right

The following is an example of custom number format that specifies a different format for each of these types:

[Green]General;[Red]General;[Black]General;[Blue]General

2.2.2   Custom number format codes

The following table lists the formatting codes available for custom formats, along with brief descriptions

Table 2.4

Code	Comments
General	Displays the number in General format
#	Digit placeholder. Does not display insignificant zeros
0 (zero)	Digit placeholder. Displays insignificant digits if a number has fewer digits than there are zeros in the format
?	Digit placeholder. Adds spaces for insignificant zeros on either side of the decimal point so that decimals points align when formatting with a fixed-width font. You can also use "?" for fractions that have varying number of digits
,	Thousands separator
$, -, +, /, (,), :, space	Displays this character
\	Displays the next character in the format
*	Repeats the next character, to fill the column width
_ (underscore)	Leaves a space equal to the width of the next character
"text"	Displays the text inside the quotation marks
@	Text placeholder
[Colour]	Displays the characters in the colour specified, can be [Black], [Blue], [Cyan], [Green], [Magenta], [Red], [White], or [Yellow]
[Condition value]	Set your own criteria for each section of a number format

Note: The default number format is General. If you prefer a different default format for your workbook, you have two choices: Preformat the cells (the whole sheet, for example) with the number format of your choice., or change the number format for the *Normal* style. Change the Normal style by displaying the Style gallery. Right-click the Normal style icon (Home Cell Style group) and choose *Modify* to display the Style dialog box. In the Style dialog box, click the Format button and then choose the new number format that you want to use for the Normal style.

The following table lists the codes that are used for creating custom formats for Dates and Times

Table 2.5

Code	Comments
m	Display the month as a number without leading zeros (1-12)
mm	Display the month as a number with leading zeros (01-12)
mmm	Display the month as an abbreviation (Jan-Dec)
mmmm	Display the month as a full name (January – December)
d	Displays the day as a number without leading zeros (1-31)
dd	Displays the day as a number with leading zeros (01-31)
ddd	Displays the day as an abbreviation (Sun – Sat)
dddd	Displays the full name of the day (Sunday– Saturday)
yy or yyyy	Displays the year as two-digit number (00 – 99) or as four-digit number (1900 – 9999)
h or hh	Displays the hour as a number without leading zeros (0 – 23) or with leading zeros (00 -23)
m or mm	When used with a colon in a time format, displays the minute as a number without leading zeros (0 – 59) or as a number with leading zeros (00 – 59)
s or ss	Displays the second as a number without leading zeros (0 – 59) or as a number with leading zeros (00 – 59)
[]	Display hours greater than 24 or minutes or seconds greater than 60
AM / PM	Displays the hour using a 12-hour clock; if no AM/PM indicator is used, the hour uses a 24-hour clock

2.3   Custom Number Format Examples

The remainder of this section consists of useful examples of custom number formats. You can use most of these format codes as is. Others may need some slight modifications.

2.3.1   Scaling values

For very large numbers you can scale them. For example, you can display numbers in thousands (such as displaying 1,200,000 as 1,200).

The following format string displays values without the last three digits to the right of the decimal place and no decimal places. In other words, the value appears as if it is divided by 1,000 and rounded to no decimal places:

#. ###, (the last character is a comma)

Table 2.6 shows examples of these number formats:

Table 2.6

Value	Number Format	Display
123456	#, ###,	123
1234567	#, ###,	1,235
-323434	#, ###,	-323
123123.123	#, ###,	123
499	#, ###,	(blank)
500	#, ###,	1
123456	#, ###.00,	123.46
1234567	#, ###.00,	1,234.57
-323434	#, ###.00,	-323.43
123123.123	#, ###.00,	123.12
499	#, ###.00,	.50
500	#, ###.00,	.50

The following format string displays values in millions with no decimal places. A value with this number format appears as if it is divided by 1,000,000 and rounded to no decimal places:

#, ###,, (last two characters are commas)

A variation of this format follows. A value with this format appears as if it is divided by 1,000,000 and rounded to two decimal places:

#,###.00,,

The following adds the letter M to the end of the value:

#,###,,M

Example: 123456789 formatted as #, ###,,M will display 123M

Example: 123456789 formatted as #, ###.00,,M will display 123.45M

2.3.2 Displaying leading zeros

To display leading zeros, create a custom number format that uses the 0 character. For example, if you want all numbers to display with ten digits, use the format **0000000000** (ten zeros). Therefore 12345 using this format will display as 0000012345. You can also force all numbers to display with a fixed number of leading zeros. A format string such as **"000"** # appends three zeros to the beginning of each number.

Example 12345 formatted as "000"# will be displayed as 00012345

2.3.3 Specifying conditions

The following custom number format displays text, based on the value of the cell:

[<10]"Too low"; [>10]"Too high"; "Just right"

2.3.4 Displaying fractions

Excel supports quite a few built-in fraction number formats in the fraction category on the number tab in the Format Cells dialog box as shown in Figure 2.3 below:

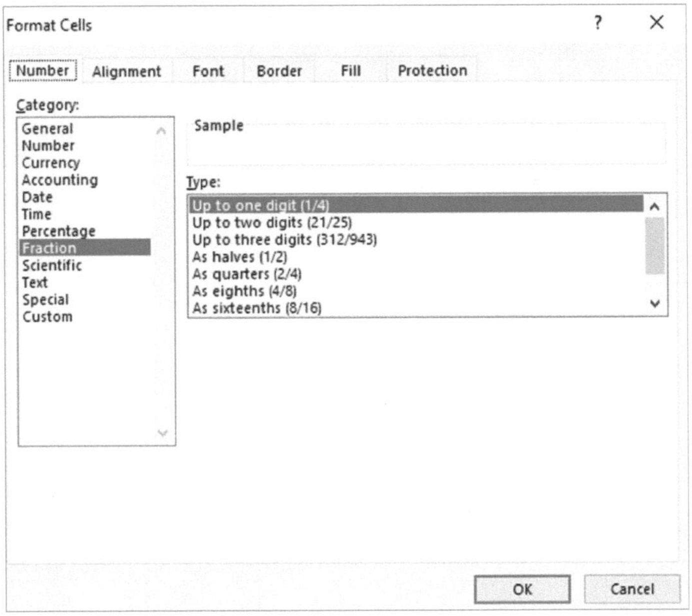

Figure 2.3

2.3.5 Formatting dates and times

Excel provides many built-in date and time formats. Table 2.7 shows some other date and time formats. The first column of the table shows the date/time serial number:

Table 1.7

Value	Number Format	Display
41456	mmmm d, yyyy (dddd)	July 1, 2013 (Monday)
41456	"It's " dddd!	It's Monday
41456	dddd, mm/dd/yyyy	Monday, 07/01/2013

41456	"Month: " mmm	Month: July
41456	General (m/d/yyyy)	41456 (7/01/2013)
0.345	h "Hours"	8 Hours
0.345	h:mm "o'clock"	8:16 o'clock
0.345	h:mm a/p "m"	8:16 am
0.78	h:mm a/p".m."	6:43 p.m.

2.3.6 Displaying text with numbers

To add text to a number, just create the number format string as usual and put the text within quotation marks:

Example: #,##0.00 "(US Dollars)" will display something like **1,234.78 (US Dollars)**

Example: "Average: "0.00 e.g. **Average 6.44**

Exercises:

Open **a new Excel** workbook. On sheet1 write a formula to display today's date in cell A1. Use the **Date** category on the Format Cells dialog to format the date as **Wednesday, 14 March 2016.** Now use the Custom format category to format the cell as **Today's date is: 14 March 2012 (Wednesday)**

Enter 1234567 in cell B1. Format it to display $1234.57. Reformat the cell to display $1.23M

Enter 421897322 in cell C1. Format it to display: ABN: 421-89-7322

Format cell D1 as follows:

If you enter 123456.789 will be displayed as 123456.790 in green

If you enter -123456.789 will be displayed as (123456.890) (in red, within blakets)

If you enter zero, the cell will be blank

If you enter your surname (text) will display "Cell must be number"

Format cell E1 such that if you enter number that is less than 10 digits, the cell will fill with leading zeros.

Format cell F1 such that numeric entry will be preceded by "000"

Format cell G1 so that your first name will be displayed as Dear xxxxxx

Enter 78.25 in cell H1. Format it to display 78 ¼

In cell I1 enter 10.75 as a fraction

3. Using Data validation

Data validation enables you to add rules for what is acceptable in specific cells and allows you to add dynamic elements to your worksheet without using any macro programming.

3.1   About Data Validation

The Excel *data validation* feature allows you to set up rules that dictates what can be entered into a cell. And to provide warning messages if the rule is violated.

3.2   Specifying Validation Criteria

To specify a data validation rule:

1. Select the cell or range
2. Choose **Data** ⟹ **Data Tools** ⟹ **Data Validation**

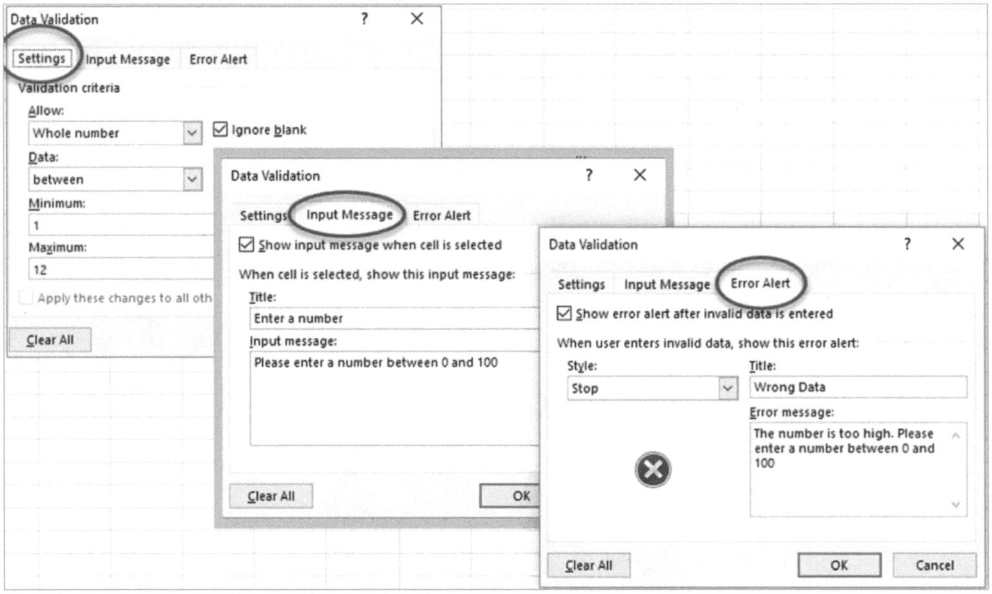

Figure 3.1

Figure 1: The three tabs of the Data Validation dialog box

3. Select the **Settings** tab
4. Choose an option from the **Allow:** drop-down list
5. Specify the condition in the controls
6. (Optional) Select the **Input Message** tab and specify a message to be displayed when a user selects the cell
7. (Optional) Select the **Error Alert** tab and specify an error message to display for an invalid entry and click OK

The Settings tab of the Data Validation dialog box contains two other check boxes:

- **Ignore Blanks**: If selected blank entries are allowed

- **Apply These Changes to All Other Cells with the Same Settings**: If selected, any changes are applied to all other cells that contain the original data validation criteria.

3.3   Experimenting with the Validation Criteria

From the **Settings** tab of the Data Validation dialog, you can specify a wide variety of data validation criteria: Experiment with them.

3.4   Creating a Drop-Down List

Drop-down list can be used as a means of restricting data in a cell.

To create a drop-down list in a cell:

1. Select the cell that will contain the drop-down list
2. Choose **Data ⇨ Data Tools ⇨ Data Validation**. The Data Validation dialog box appears
3. From the **Settings** tab, select the **List** option (from the **Allow:** drop-down list)
4. In the Source text box, enter the values, separated by commas (e.g. "Jan", "Feb", "Mar",…). You can also select the source from a range
5. Select the **In-Cell Dropdown** check box
6. Set any other data validation options and click OK

3.5   Using Formulas for Data Validation Rules

The real power of data validation is in data validation formulas. The formula must be a logical formula that returns either **TRUE** or **FALSE**. A formula that returns TRUE considers the data to be valid. You specify a formula in the Data Validation dialog box by selecting the Custom option from the Allow drop-down list of the Settings tab. Enter the formula directly into the formula control, or enter a reference to a cell that contains a formula.

3.6   Understanding Cell References

If a formula that is entered into the Data Validation dialog box contains references, that reference is considered a relative reference, based on the upper-left cell in the selected range.

As an example, to allow only odd numbers in range A1:A10, after selecting range A1:A10 with cell A1 as the active cell, you will enter the following formula:

=ISODD(A1). Notice that the formula references only the active cell in the range

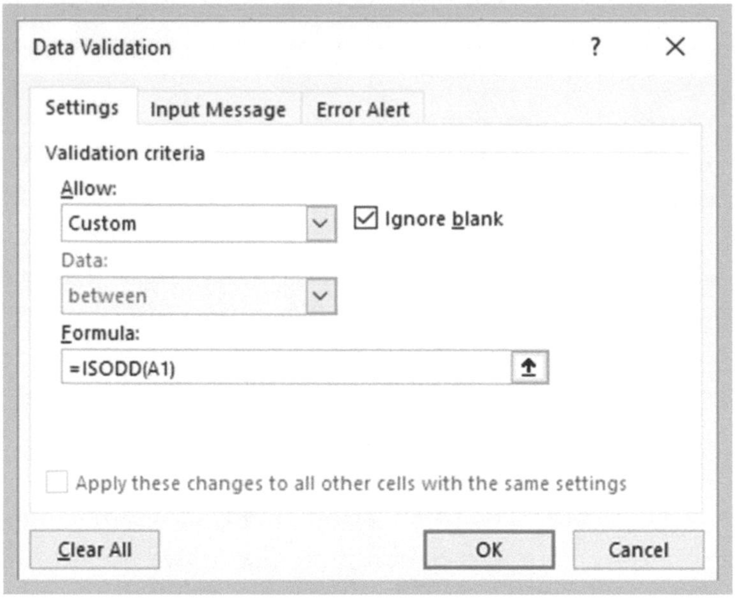

Figure 3.2: Data Validation Formula

3.7 Data Validation Formula Examples
The following examples may enlighten you to create your own data validation formulas.

3.7.1 Accepting text only
Cells accept only text:

Example: =ISTEXT(A1) where A1 refers to the active cell in a selected target range

3.7.2 Accepting larger value than the previous cell
The following formula accepts only values in a cell that are larger than the cell directly above it:

=A2>A1

This formula assumes that A2 is the active cell in the selected range. You cannot use this formula for a cell in row 1 (the formula A1>A0 is not valid)

3.7.3 Accepting non-duplicate entries only
The following data validation formula does not allow the user to make a duplicate entry into the range A1:C20:

=COUNTIF($A$1:$C$20,A1)=1

This is a logical formula that returns TRUE if the value in the cell occurs only one time in the A1:C20 range. Otherwise, it returns FALSE, and the Duplicate Entry dialog box is displayed. This formula assumes that A1 is the active cell in the selected range. Note that the first argument for COUNTIF is an absolute reference. The second argument in the formula above is relative reference, it adjusts for each cell in the validation range.

3.7.4 Accepting text that begins with a specific character

The following data validation formula demonstrates how to check for a specific character. In this case, the formula ensures that the user's entry is a text string that begins with the letter A

=LEFT(A1)="a"

This is a logical formula that returns TRUE if the first character in the cell is the letter A. Otherwise, it returns FALSE. This formula assumes that the active cell in the selected range is cell A1

The following formula is a variation of this validation formula. It uses wildcard characters in the second argument of the COUNTIF function. In this case, the formula ensures that the entry begin with the letter A and contains exactly five characters:

=COUNTIF(A1,"A?????")=1

3.7.5 Accepting dates by the day of the week

The following data validation formula ensures that the cell entry is a date, and that the date is a Monday:

WEEKDAY(A1)=2

This formula assumes that the active cell in the selected range is cell A3. The WEEKDAY function returns 1 for Sunday, 2 for Monday and so on.

3.7.6 Accepting only values that don't exceed a total

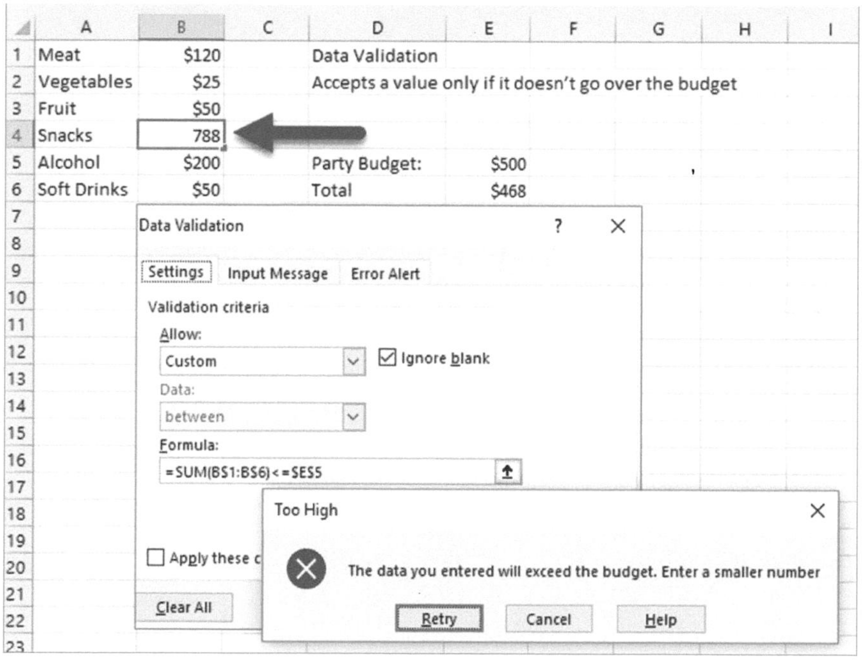

Figure 3.3

Figure 3.3 shows a simple budget worksheet, with the budget item amount in the range B1:B6. The planned budget is in cell E5, and the user is attempting to enter a value in cell B4 that would cause the total (cell E6) to exceed the budget. The following data validation formula ensures that the sum of the budget items does not exceed the budget:

SUM($B$1:$B$6)<=$E$5

3.7.7 Creating a dependent list

You can use a dropdown list to control the entries that appear in a second dropdown list. Figure 3.4 shows a simple example of a dependent list created by using data validation. Cell E2 contains data validation that displays a three-item list from the range A1:C1 (Vegetables, Fruits, and Meats). When the user chooses an item from the list, the second list (in cell F2) displays the appropriate items.

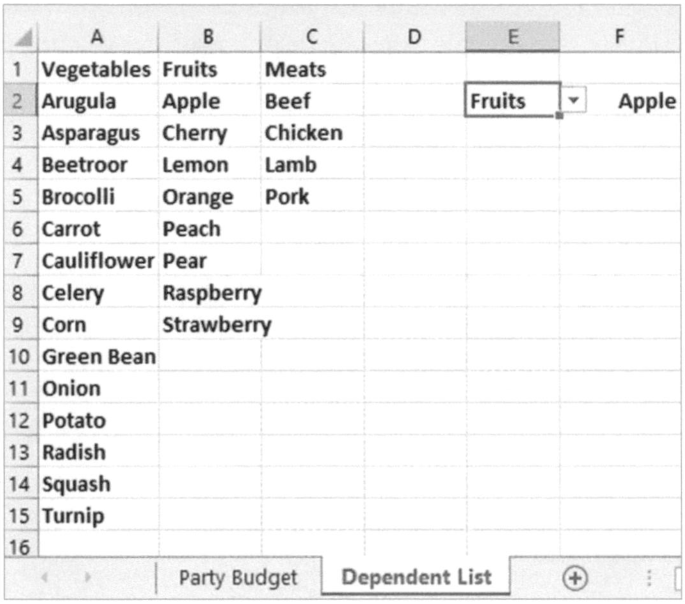

	A	B	C	D	E	F
1	Vegetables	Fruits	Meats			
2	Arugula	Apple	Beef		Fruits ▾	Apple
3	Asparagus	Cherry	Chicken			
4	Beetroor	Lemon	Lamb			
5	Brocolli	Orange	Pork			
6	Carrot	Peach				
7	Cauliflower	Pear				
8	Celery	Raspberry				
9	Corn	Strawberry				
10	Green Bean					
11	Onion					
12	Potato					
13	Radish					
14	Squash					
15	Turnip					
16						

Party Budget   Dependent List   ⊕

Figure 3.4

This worksheet uses three named ranges:

- Vegetables: A2:A15
- Fruits: B2:B9
- Meats: C2:C5

Cell F2 contains data validation that uses this formula:

=INDIRECT($E$2)

Therefore, the dropdown list displayed in F2 depends on the value displayed in cell E2

EXERCISE

Create a new workbook as shown in Figure 5.3. Enter the data exactly as shown in range C2:G8. Enter "Continent" in cell I2 and "Country" in cell K2. In cell I3, create a dropdown list to show the continents. In cell K3, create a dropdown list to show only the countries for the continent shown in cell I3.

Hint:

- Use range C2:G2 (a list) as source for cell I3 data validation

- Create names for each continent (Values: countries for each continent)

You can select range C2:G8, then use **Formulas Define Names Create from Selection**

- Cell K3 Validation: List (Source: INDIRECT($I$3)

	A	B	C	D	E	F	G	H	I	J	K
1											
2			Africa	Europe	Australia	Americas	Asia		Continent		Country
3			Ghana	UK	Australia	USA	China		Africa		Ghana
4			Nigeria	Germany	Fiji	Canada	India				
5			Egypt	France	PNG		Argentina	Malaysia			
6			Cote'Devo	Belgium		Brazil					
7				Sweden		Peru					
8				Finland		Colombia					

Figure 3.5

4.   Creating and Using Worksheet Outlines

Worksheet outlines allows you to collapse (to show only summary data) or expand (to show details and summary worksheet data). Outlines are ideal for creating reports for different levels of management.

4.1   Creating an Outline

There are two ways to create worksheet outlines: automatically and manually. Before creating an outline, the data must be appropriate for outlines and formulas must be set up properly.

4.1.1   Preparing the data

Generally, data fit for outlines should be hierarchical such as:

Company

   Division

      Department

         Budget Category (e.g. travel expenses)

            Budget Item (e.g. Airfare, hotel expenses)

The data arrangement suitable for an outline is essentially a summary table of the data. All summary formulas must be entered correctly and consistently. For example, summary formulas, such as subtotals, must be either below the data to which they refer, or above the referenced cells.

> *Note: If summary formulas are not consistent (some are above and some are below the data), you still can create an outline, but has to be done manually. Also if the data is a table, outline has to be created manually.*

4.1.2   Creating an outline automatically

To have Excel create an outline:

- Move the cell pointer anywhere within the range of data that is to be outlined
- Choose **Data Outline Group Auto Outline**

Depending on the formulas that you have, Excel creates a row outline, a column outline, or both.

> *Note: Excel automatically creates an outline when you choose Data Outline Subtotal which inserts subtotal formulas automatically*

4.1.3   Creating an outline manually

If any of the following conditions apply to the data, Excel cannot create outlines automatically; Outline must be created manually:

- Some subtotals are above the data and some are below
- The data does not contain any summary formulas

Creating an outline manually consists of creating groups of rows (for row outline) or groups of columns (for column outline)

To create an outline manually:

- Select the rows to be included in the group
- Choose **Data Outline Group Group**
- Repeat this process for each group to be included in the outline

Exercise: Create an outline with the data in Sheet1 of the outline.xlsx workbook

4.2   Working with outlines

The following information explain the basic operations for working with worksheet outline

4.2.1   Displaying levels

To display various outline levels, click the appropriate outline symbol. These symbols consist of buttons with numbers on them (1, 2, 3, and so on) or a plus (+) or minus (-) sign. You can expand a particular section by clicking its plus-sign button, or collapse s section using the minus-sign button.

The **Hide Detail** and **Show Detail** commands (**Data Outline**) can be used to perform their respective functions.

4.2.2   Adding data to an outline

For an outline that was created automatically, row or column insertion or deletion can be done by choosing **Data Outline Group Auto Outline**, after inserting the data. Excel makes you verify that you want to modify the existing outline.

4.2.3   Removing an outline

To remove an outline:

Data Ungroup Clear Outline

4.2.4   Adjusting the outline symbols

When you create a manual outline, Excel puts the outline symbol below the summary row. To place the outline symbol on the same row as the summary row, follow this procedure:

- Click the dialog box launcher to the lower right of the **Data Outline group**. Excel displays the dialog box shown in Figure 4.1

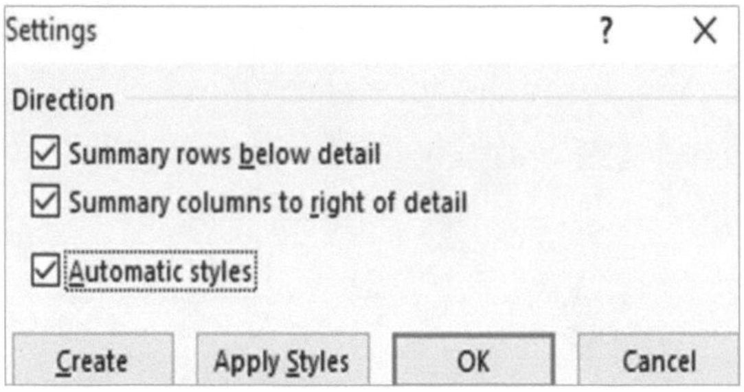

Figure 4.1

- Remove the check mark from the **Summary row below detail** option and click OK.

4.2.5   Hiding the outline symbols

You can create more screen space by removing the outline symbols without removing the outline itself. Press ctrl + 8 to toggle the outline symbol on and off. When the outline symbol is hidden, you cannot expand or collapse the outline. The Custom View feature, which saves named view of your outline, also saves the status of the outline symbols as part of view, enabling you to name some view with the outline symbols and other views without them.

5. Linking and Consolidating Worksheets

Linking is the process of using references to cells in external workbooks to get data into the current worksheet. ***Consolidation*** combines or summarizes information from two or more worksheets.

5.1 Creating External Reference Formulas

External references to a worksheet can be established in various ways:

- **Type the references manually,** including workbook and worksheet names, and even drive and path information
- **Point to the cell references.** If the source workbook is open, you can use the standard pointing technique to create formulas that use external references
- **Paste the links.** Copy the data from the source to the clipboard and paste to the destination
- Choose **Data Data Tools Consolidate**

5.1.1 Understanding link formula syntax

The general syntax for an external reference formula is:

=[WorkbookName]SheetName!CellAddress

Example: [Budget.xlsx]Sheet1!A1. If there are any spaces in the workbook name or the sheet name, the text must be enclosed in single quotation marks:

='[Annual Budget.xlsx]Sheet1'!A1

When a formula is linked to a different, closed workbook that is located in a folder other than the current folder, the complete path to the reference is required:

='C:\Data\Excel\Budget\[Annual Budget.xlsx]Sheet1'!A1

If the workbook is stored on the internet the link is established as follows:

'http://d:docs.live.net/86a6d/Documents/[Annual Budget.xlsx]Sheet1'!A1

EXERCISE

1. Open a new workbook. In cellA1, write a linked formula to display the value in cell C4 of 'C:\GrandTotals\Course Outline\GT002_Adv\Ribbon Customization.xlsx workbook.
2. Repeat exercise 1 but add 1,000 to the value and format (using the Text function) it as Dollar

5.1.2 Creating a link formula by pointing

Excel can build a linked formula as follows:

1. Open the source workbook
2. Select the cell in the dependent workbook that will hold the formula
3. Type an equal sigh (=)

4. Activate the source workbook and select the cell or range and press **Enter**

With this method of linking, Excel automatically takes care of the external references in the formula.

Note: After you close the source workbook, the external reference formula is adjusted to include the full path (or URL) to the source workbook

Exercise: Repeat exercise 1 above but this time use a linked formula by pointing

5.1.3 Pasting links

Pasting links provides another way of creating external reference formulas. This method is applicable when you simply want to reference other cells

1. Open the source workbook
2. Select the cell or range you want linked and copy to the clipboard
3. Activate the dependent workbook and select the target cells. For a range, just select the upper-left cell
4. 4. Choose **Home** ⇨ **Clipboard** ⇨ **Paste** ⇨ **Paste Link (N)**

Exercise:

Open a new workbook. Open any existing workbook and copy a range from the existing workbook into the new workbook. Paste as Link

5.2 Working with External Reference Formulas

Some security features are associated with external links. The first time you open a workbook that contains links to other files, a security warning like figure 5.1 appears. Click the ***Enable Content*** button to update the link

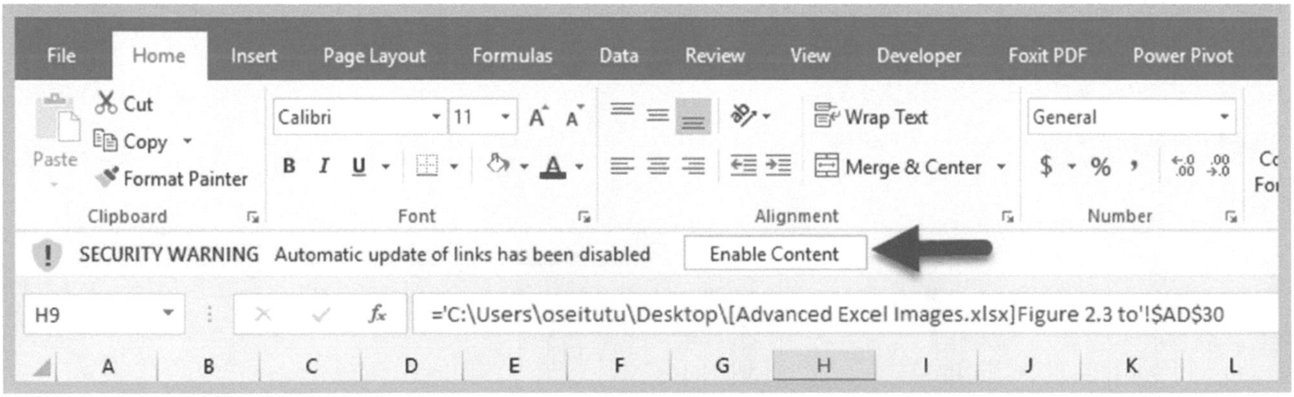

Figure 5.1

To disable the security warning, follow these steps:

1. Choose **File** ⇨ **Options**
2. Select the **Trust Centre** tab

3. Click the ***Trust Centre Settings*** button
4. Select the External Content tab, and change the option for ***Security Setting for Workbook Links***

5.2.1 Opening a workbook with external reference formulas

When you open a workbook that contains links, Excel displays a dialog box (Figure 5.2):

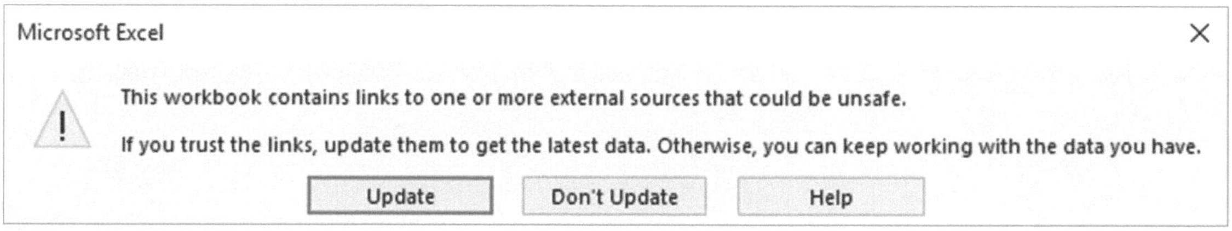

Figure 5.2

- **Update:** The links are updated with the current information in the source

- **Don't Update**: The links are not updated. Previous information still remains

Exercises:

Close both workbooks from the previous exercise. Save the new workbook on the Desktop with the default name. Open the workbook again (from the desktop). Close it again. Open the source workbook and make a change in a cell. Close the workbook. Open the dependent workbook (from the desktop). Update link

If you don't update a link when you open the dependent workbook, you can update it any time by choosing **Data ➡ Edit Links**. In the Edit Links dialog box that appears (Figure 5.3), click the link and then click Update Values.

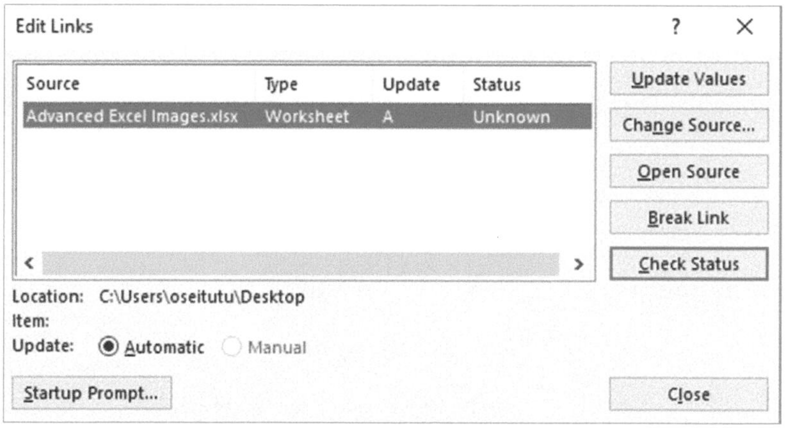

Figure 5.3

> ***Note: Figure 14 is also displayed if the source workbook is deleted or renamed when you open the destination workbook and you choose Update on the dialog box that appears (Figure 5.3). In this case, you select "Change Source"***

Exercise:

Open the destination workbook again (desktop) from the previous exercise. Close the dialog box. Use Data -> Edit Link to update the link

5.2.2 Changing the start-up prompt

When you open a workbook that contains external links, Excel, by default, displays the dialog box shown in Figure 5.3. You can eliminate this prompt by changing the settings in the Start-up prompt dialog box as shown in Figure 5.4 below:

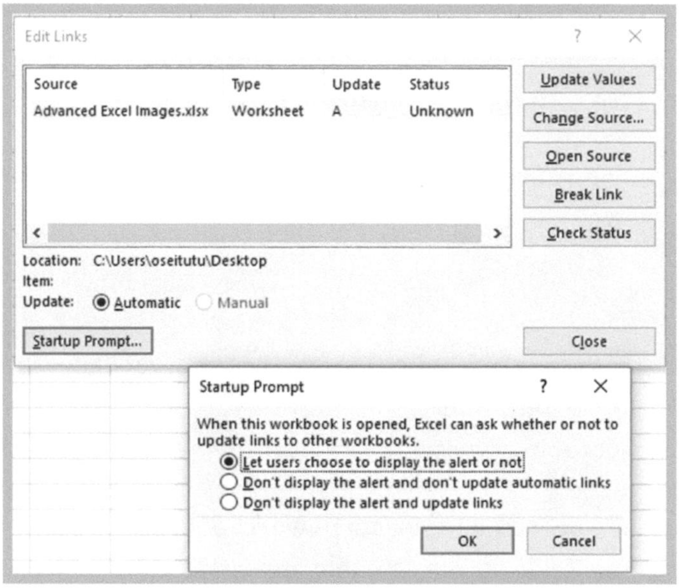

Figure 5.4

5.2.3 Updating links

To update the links in your workbook, select the appropriate source workbook (Figure 5.4) and click the **Update Values** button.

5.2.4 Changing the link source

If the data in the source workbook have been updated or you have changed the workbook name, you can use the **Change Source** button (Figure 5.4) to point the linked cells to the correct workbook

5.2.5 Severing link

If for some reason you no longer need the links from the source workbook, you can use the **Break Link** button (Figure 5.4) to sever the links. In this case you will not be prompted any more to update links.

Note: To avoid some potential problems with linked cells:

- *Always (if possible), open all dependent workbooks if you want to modify the source. In this case Excel adjusts referenced cells appropriately*
- *It is best to use named cells or named ranges. The names will always be correct in the linked formulas even if rows or columns are added to or deleted from the source worksheet.*

5.3   Consolidating Worksheets

Various methods are used in Excel to consolidate information from multiple worksheets:

- Use external reference formula
- Copy the data from the source and paste into the destination
- Use the Consolidate dialog box, which is reached by choosing **Data Data Tools Consolidate**

5.3.1   Consolidating worksheets by using formulas

This simply involves creating formulas that use references to other worksheets or workbooks. With this methods, the referencing cells are updated automatically when values in the source cells change. In addition, the source workbooks don't need to be open when you create the consolidation formulas.

If you are consolidating the worksheets in the same workbook and all the worksheets are laid out identically, you can just use standard formulas to create the consolidation. For example, to compute the totals for cell A1 in worksheets named Sheet2 through Sheet10, enter the following formula:

=SUM(Sheet2:Sheet10!A1)

If the consolidation involves other workbooks, you can use external reference formula to perform the consolidation. For example, if you want to add the values in cell A1 from Sheet1 in two different workbooks (named Zone1 and Zone2), you can use the following formula

=[Zone1.xlsx]Sheet1!A1 +[Zone2.xlsx]Sheet1!A1

5.3.2   Consolidating worksheets by Using Paste Special

The **Paste Special** dialog box can perform a mathematical operation when it pastes data from the keyboard. For example, you can use the **Add** option to add the copied data to the values in the selected range. This method is applicable only when all the worksheets are open. This method is not dynamic. The results are static

To consolidate by this method:

1. Copy the data from the source range
2. Activate the dependent workbook and select a location for the consolidated data. A single cell is sufficient
3. Choose **Home** ⇒ **Clipboard** ⇒ **Paste Special**. The Paste Special dialog box appears
4. Choose the **Add** option, and click **OK**

Repeat the process for each source range that you want to consolidate, making sure that the consolidation location in Step 2 is the same for each paste operation.

5.3.3 Consolidating worksheets by using the Consolidate dialog box

For the ultimate in data consolidation, use the **Consolidate** dialog box. The consolidation can result in static (no link formulas) or dynamic (with link formulas). The Data Consolidation feature supports the following methods of consolidation:

- **By position**: With this method, Excel consolidates the data from several worksheets using the same range coordinates on each sheet. This method is accurate only if the worksheets have an identical layout

- **By category**: This method tells Excel to consolidate the data by looking for identical row and column labels in each sheet. For example, if one worksheet lists monthly computer sales in row 1 and another lists computer sales in row 5, you can still consolidate as long as both sheets have a "**Computer Sales**" label at the beginning of these rows

In both cases, you specify one or more *source ranges* (the ranges that have the data you want to consolidate) and a *destination range* (the range where the consolidated data will appear)

5.3.4 A workbook consolidation example

Consolidate by position:

If the sheets you're working with have the same layout, consolidation by position is the way to go. For example, the worksheets **Division I Budget, Division II Budget, and Division III Budget** all have identical layout (row and column labels)

To consolidate the three worksheets:

1. Open the three referencing workbooks
2. Create a new worksheet with row and column labels as the sheets you are consolidating
3. Select the upper-left corner of the new (destination) worksheet. In this example, cell B4
4. Select **Data ⇒ Consolidate**. Excel displays the **Consolidate** dialog box
5. In the **Function** dropdown list, ensure the **SUM** function is selected
6. Select the Referencing test box
7. Click on the **View** tab in the Ribbon and select the Division1 Budget workbook
8. Select the data in range **B4:M17** and click **Add** on the Consolidate dialog box
9. Repeat steps 4 and 5 to add all the source ranges using the **Division II Budget** and **Division III Budget** workbooks
10. For a dynamic consolidation, select the **Create Links to Source Data** check box

If you create links, Excel:

- Adds link formula to the destination range for each cell in the source range you selected

- Consolidates the data using the aggregate function you used (e.g. SUM)

- Outlines the consolidation worksheet and hides the link formula

Exercise:

In the **Consolidation_Example** worksheet, in cell **A2,** consolidate the Expenses data in the "**Office Records**" sheet using the following ranges: **A10:B23**; **E10:F23**; **A30:B43**; **E30:F43**; **A50:B63**; **E50:F63** and **A70:B83**. Use the **SUM** function for the consolidation and add labels from the left column.1

6. Protecting Your Work

A worksheet may be protected to prevent accidental deletion of formulas or data. Protection can also prevent worksheets from being overwritten or copied.

6.1 Types of Protection

Excel's protection-related features fall into three categories:

- **Worksheet protection**: Protecting a worksheet from being modified or restricting the modifications to certain users

- **Workbook protection**: Preventing insertion of sheets into and deletion of sheets from a workbook and requiring the use of a password to open the workbook

- **Visual Basic (VB) protection**: Using a password to prevent others from viewing or modifying the VBA code

6.2 Protecting a Worksheet

To protect a worksheet:

- Activate the worksheet and choose **Review** ⇨ **Changes** ⇨ **Protect Sheet**. Excel displays the Protect Sheet dialog box shown in Figure 6.1.

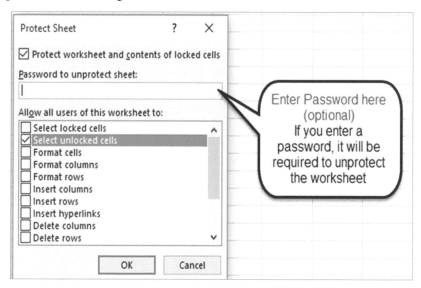

Figure 6.1

6.2.1 Unlocking cells

By default, all cells in a worksheet are locked. Every cell has a **Locked** attribute which determines whether the cell can be changed when the sheet is protected.

To change the **Locked** attribute, follow these steps:

1. Select the cells or range that you wish to unlock (all cells are locked by default)
2. Click **Home** ⇨ **Cells** ⇨ **Format**

3. On the dropdown menu click **Lock Cell**

After the cells are unlocked, choose **Review** ⇒ **Changes** ⇒ **Protect Sheet** to protect the sheet

The cell or range will not be locked until the sheet is protected

6.2.2   Sheet protection options

Excel allows many options for protected sheets as shown in Figure 6.2 below. These options are self-explanatory. For example, the option **"Select Locked Cells"**, allows the user to select (but not modify) a cell that is locked.

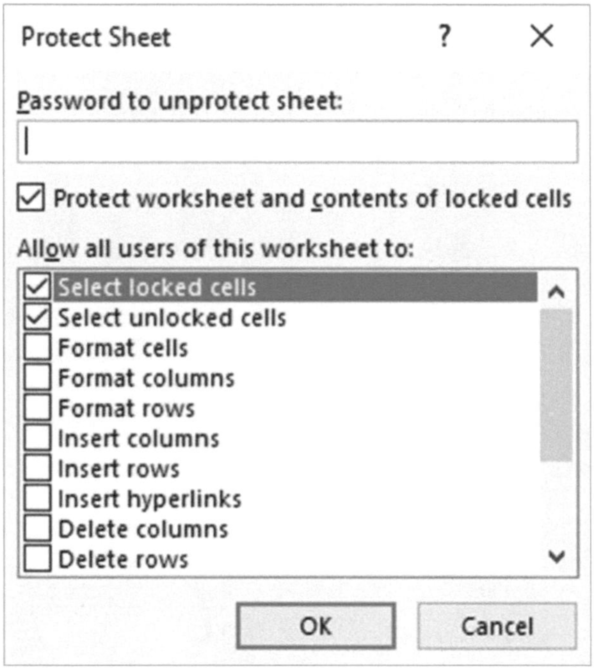

Figure 6.2

6.2.3   Assigning user permissions

You can assign user-level permissions to different areas on a protected worksheet. You can specify which users can edit which range while the worksheet is protected. As an option you can require a password to make changes.

To set up user-assigned permissions:

1. Unprotect the sheet if it is protected
2. Choose **Review** ⇒ **Changes group** ⇒ **Allow Users to Edit Ranges**. The dialog box shown in Figure 6.3 below is displayed

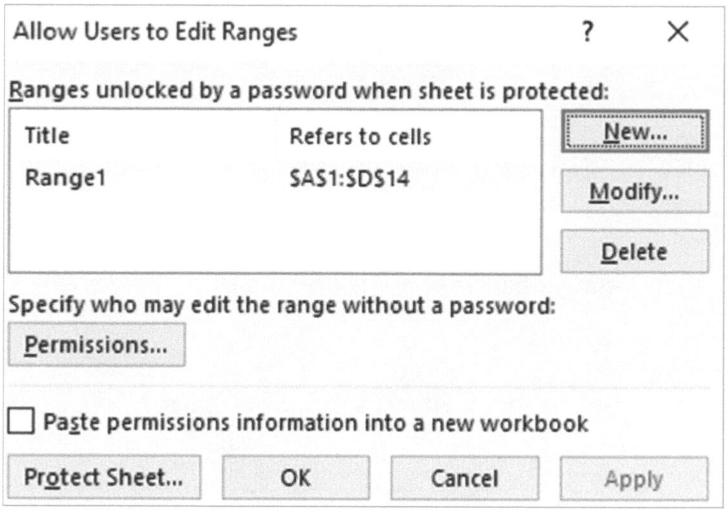

Figure 6.3

3. Click the **New** button and follow the prompts in the series of dialog boxes the follow
4. Protect the sheet

6.3 Protecting a Workbook

There are two ways to protect a workbook in Excel:

- Protection that requires a password to open a workbook

- Protection that prevent users from adding, deleting, hiding, and un-hiding sheets

6.3.1 Requiring a password to open a workbook

If you save a workbook with a password, that password will be required to open the workbook

To add a password to a workbook:

1. Choose **File ⇒ Info ⇒ Protect Workbook ⇒ Encrypt with Password**

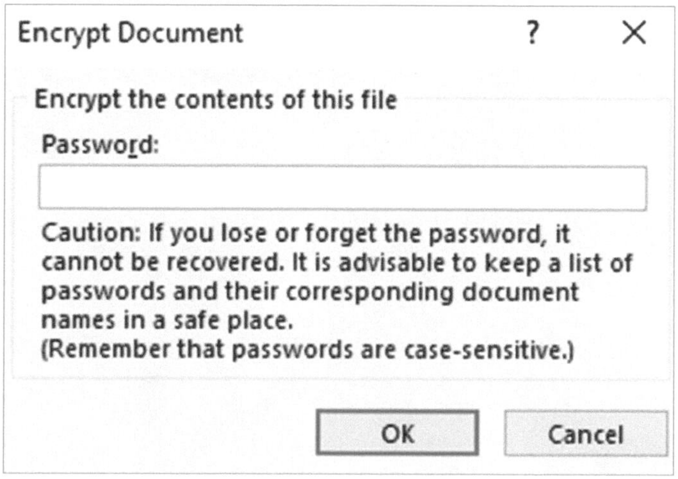

Figure 6.4

2. Type a password and click OK (Figure 6.4)
3. Confirm the password from step 2
4. Save the workbook

To remove a password from a workbook, repeat the above procedure. In step 2, however, delete the existing password you entered into the password textbox (Figure 6.4), click OK and save

An alternative approach of providing a password for a workbook:

1. Choose **File** ➡ **Save As**
2. Click the **Tools** button and choose **General Options (Figure 6.5)**

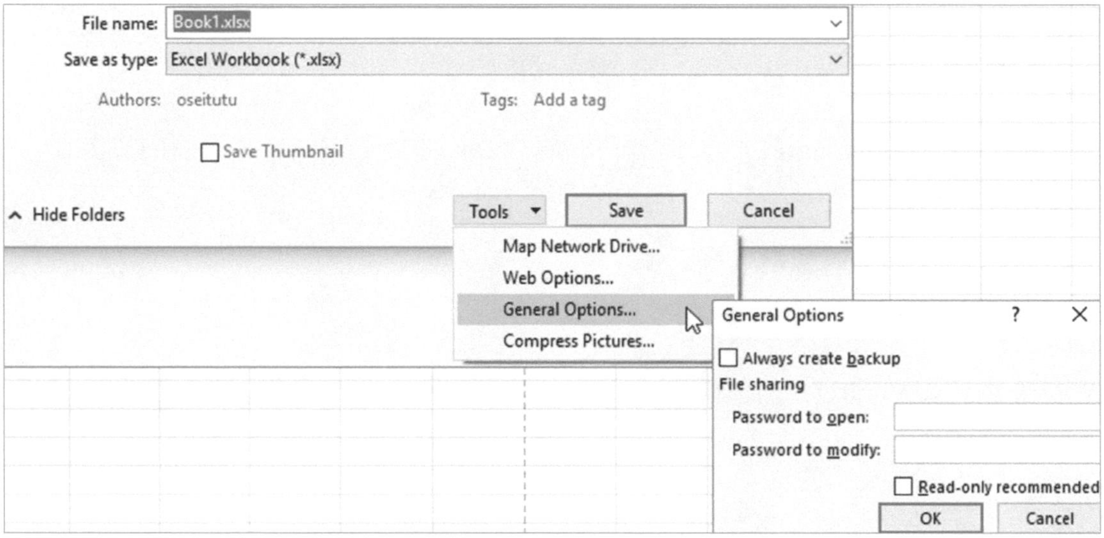

Figure 6.5

3. Enter a password in the **Password to Open** textbox and click OK
4. In the **Save As** dialog box, make sure the filename, location, and type are correct; then click **Save**

6.3.2   Protecting a workbook's structure

When the structure of a workbook is protected, users may not:

- Add a sheet
- Delete a sheet
- Hide a sheet
- Unhide a sheet
- Rename a sheet
- Move a sheet

To protect a workbook's structure:

1. Choose **Review** ➡ **Changes group** ➡ **Protect Workbook**. The dialog box (Figure 6.6) is shown

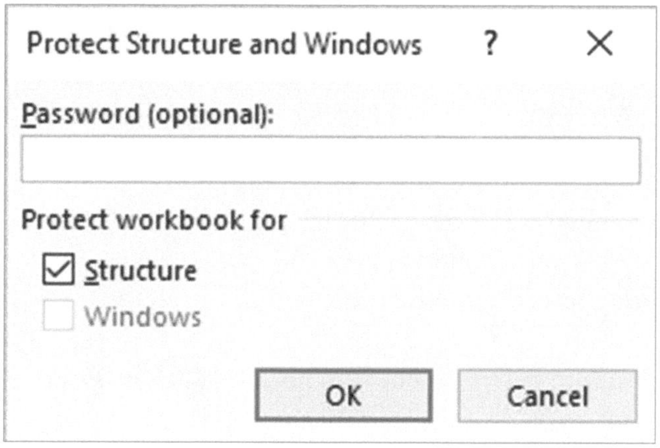

Figure 6.6

2. Select the **Structure** checkbox as shown
3. (Optional) Enter a password
4. Click **OK**

To unprotect the workbook's structure, choose **Review ⇒ Changes ⇒ Unprotect Workbook**

6.4 VB Project Protection

If the workbook contains any VBA macros, you may want to protect the VB project to prevent others from viewing or modifying your macros. To protect a VB project:

1. Press **Alt + F11** to activate the VB Editor
2. Select your project in the project window
3. Choose **Tools *<Project Name>* Properties**
4. Select the **Protection** tab
5. Select the **Lock Project for Viewing** check box
6. Enter a password (twice)
7. Click OK and save your file

6.5 Related Topics

Excel allows other ways to protect and distribute workbooks

Exercise

Open the ***Protect Worksheet.xlsx*** workbook. Protect only the formula cells on Sheet1 (leave nonformula cells unprotected)

6.5.1 Saving a worksheet as a PDF file

A Workbook can be saved in PDF or XPS format:

Choose **Files ⇒ Export ⇒ Create PDF/XPS**. Specify a filename and location to save the file

6.5.2 Marking a workbook final

Excel allows you to mark a workbook as final. This action produces the following outcome to the workbook:

- It makes the workbook read-only so that the file can't be saved using the same name
- It makes the workbook view-only so that it cannot be modified

When you open a finalized workbook, you see a message below the Ribbon. You can override its final status by clicking the **Edit Anyway** button. If you decide to edit a finalized workbook, it loses its finalized status and you must repeat the process to make it a final document again.

To finalize a workbook, choose **File Info Protect Workbook Mark as Final**. A dialog box appears, where you can confirm your choice

6.6.3 Inspecting a workbook

Workbook inspection allows you to highlight hidden and personal information in the workbook so you can decide to remove information that you do not want to share before you distribute the workbook.

To inspect a workbook:

1. Choose **File Info Check for Issues Inspect Document.** The Document Inspector dialog box, shown in Figure 6.7 appears
2. Click **Inspect**. Excel displays the results of the inspection and gives you the opportunity to remove the items it finds

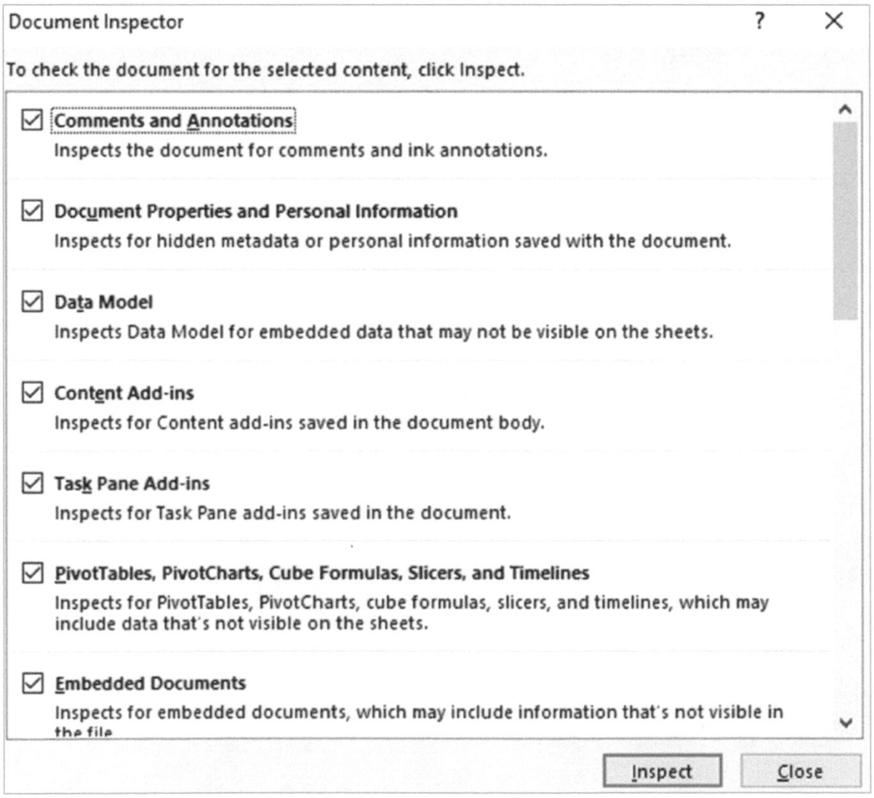

Figure 6.7

7.   Making a Workbook Error Free

In this part of the course we look at how to identify, correct, and prevent errors

Errors in Excel tend to fall into these categories:

- **Syntax errors**: For example, a formula may have misplaced parenthesis, a function may not have the correct number of arguments

- **Logical errors**: A formula doesn't return an error, but it contains a logical flaw that causes it to return an incorrect result

- **Incorrect reference errors**: The logic of the formula is correct, but the formula uses an incorrect cell reference. For example, the range reference for a Sum function may not include all the data required

- **Semantic errors**: For example, an incorrectly spelt function name. This will cause the #Name? error

- **Circular reference:** This occurs when a formula for a cell makes reference to that same cell

- **Array formula entry error:** Failure to press the **Ctrl + Shift + Enter** key combination for array formulas may result in an error or incorrect result

- **Incomplete calculation errors**: The formulas simply aren't calculated fully. To ensure the formulas are fully calculated, **press Ctrl + Alt + Shift + F9**

Mismatched parenthesis error comes in two forms: unequal number of left and right parenthesis and misplaced parenthesis. The first type will immediately produce an error message. The second type might not produce an error message but will give an incorrect result. The following formula correctly converts the first character of a text to uppercase and the rest of the characters to lowercase:

=UPPER(LEFT(A1)) & RIGHT(LOWER(A1), LEN(A1)-1)

The following is the same formula but with a misplaced parenthesis. The result is that all characters in the text are shown in uppercase:

=UPPER(LEFT(A1) & RIGHT(LOWER(A1), LEN(A1)-1))

A cell is filled with a series of hash marks (#) for two reasons:

- The column is too narrow for the cell value
- The cell contains a formula that returns an invalid date or time

If you press the spacebar in a cell that contains something, the content of the cell is replaced with an invisible character and the cell is not really blank. Any formula that includes such a cell will produce a wrong result if the formula expects the cell to be truly blank. You can use the **Find and Replace** dialog box to find all cells with a hidden space character by searching for * * (asterisk, space, asterisk)

7.1.4   Formula returning an error
A formula may return any of the following error values:

- #DIV/0!
- #N/A
- #NAME?
- #NULL!
- #NUM!
- #REF!
- #VALUE!

7.1.4.1   #DIV/0! Errors
Mathematically, a division by zero produces an infinity and Excel expresses this with this error. If a data is not available for a formula, Excel assumes that the empty cell contains zero in any formula that involves that cell. To avoid this kind of error, use the IFERROR function to check if the divisor cell is blank or zero:

=IFERROR(*value, value_if_error*)

7.1.4.2   #N/A errors
The **#N/A** error occurs if any cell referenced by a formula displays #N/A. For example, this error can occur when a lookup function (**HLOOKUP, VLOOKUP, MATCH**, or **LOOKUP**) can't find a match. If you wish to display an empty string instead of the #N/A use the IFNA function:

=IFNA(VLOOKUP(A1, C1:F50, 4, FALSE), "")

7.1.4.3   #Name? errors
The #NAME? error occurs under these conditions:

- The formula contains an undefined range or cell name
- The formula contains text that Excel interprets as an undefined name; for example, a misspelled function name
- The formula contains test that is not enclosed in quotation marks
- The formula contains a range reference that omits the colon between the cell addresses, such as **A1 A10** instead of **A1:A10**
- The formula uses a worksheet function that is defined in an add-in, and the add-in is not installed

7.1.4.4   #NULL! Errors
A #NULL! Error occurs when a formula attempts to use an intersection of two ranges that don't actually intersect. You also get this error if you omit an operator in a formula. For example, the following formula is missing the second operator:

=A1+A2 A3

This error occurs when:

- You pass a nonnumeric argument to a function when a numeric argument is expected. For example, passing $1,000 (string) instead of 1000

- You pass an invalid argument to a function, such as passing a negative argument to the square root function (SQRT)

- A formula returns a value that is too large or too small. Excel supports values between

-1E-307 and 1E+307

7.1.4.6 #REF! errors

This error occurs when a formula uses an invalid cell reference. The error can occur in the following situations:

- You delete the row or column of a cell that is referenced by a formula

- You delete the worksheet of a cell that is referenced by the formula. For example, if sheet2 is deleted, the following formula produces the #Ref! error:

  =Sheet2!A1

- You copy a formula to a location that invalidates the relative cell reference. For example, if you copy the following formula from cell A2 to cell A1, the formula returns #Ref! because an attempt is made to reference a non-existent cell: A1-1 (the formula becomes A0-1)

- You cut a cell to the clipboard and then paste it to a cell that's referenced by a formula. The formula will display #Ref!

7.1.4.7 #VALUE? Errors

A **#VALUE**! Error is very common and can occur under the following conditions:

- An argument for a function is of an incorrect data type, or a formula attempts to perform an operation using incorrect data. For example, a formula that adds a numeric value to text string returns the #VALUE! Error

- A function argument is a range when it should be a single value

- A custom worksheet function is not calculated. You can press **Ctrl + Alt + F9** to force a recalculation

- A custom worksheet function attempts to perform an operation that is not valid. For example, custom functions can't modify the Excel environment or make changes to other cells

- You forgot to press **Ctrl + Shift + Enter** when entering an array formula.

7.1.5 Absolute/relative reference problems

If a particular cells needs to be referenced in a formula even when the formula is copied to other cells, the referenced cell must be absolute.

7.1.6 Operator precedence problems

It is usually best to use parentheses in formulas that may cause problem and confusing without them. For example, a formula such as =1 + (A1*A2) is much clearer than =1+A1*A2

7.2 Using Excel Auditing Tools

Excel comes with many tools that can help with tracking formula errors.

7.2.1 Identifying cells of a particular type

The **Go To Special** dialog box (Figure 7.1) is a tool that enables you to locate cells of a particular type. To display this dialog box, choose **Home** ➡ **Editing** ➡ **Find & Select** ➡ **Go To Special…**

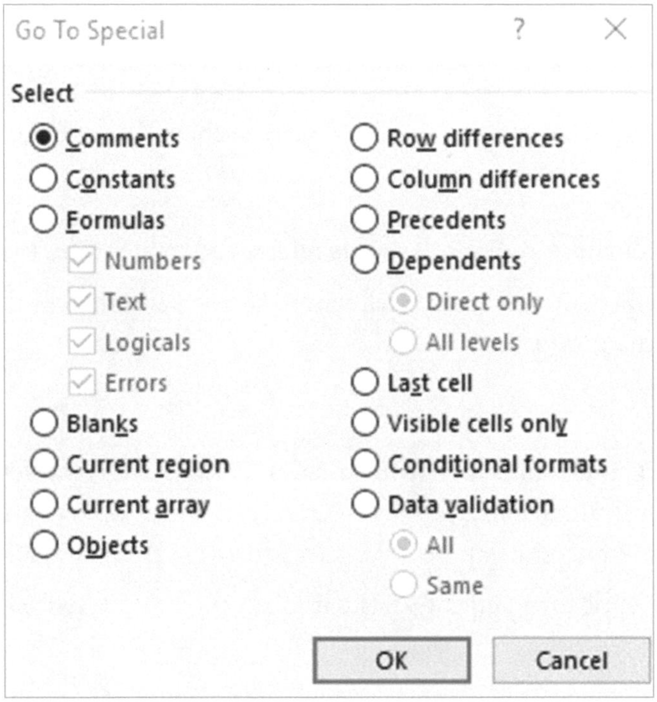

Figure 7.1

You can use the Go To Special dialog, box to select cells of a certain type, which can often help to identify errors. For example, if you choose the **Formula** option, Excel selects all the cells that contain a formula.

7.2.2 Viewing formulas

You can become familiar with a worksheet by displaying the formulas rather than the results of the formulas. To toggle the display of formulas, choose **Formulas** ➡ **Formula Auditing** ➡ **Show Formulas**. It is best to create a second window of the workbook before issuing this command. This way, you can see the formula in one window and the results of the formula in the other window. Choose **View** ➡ **Window** ➡ **New Window** to open a new window.

Figure 7.2 shows an example of a worksheet displayed in two windows. The window on the left shows a normal view (formula results), and the window on the right displays the formulas for the cells of the workbook on the left

	January	February	March
Expense Budget Calculation			
INCREAS 1.03			
EXPENS January	February	March	
Advertisi 4,600	4,200	5,200	
Rent 2,100	2,100	2,100	
Supplies 1,300	1,200	1,400	
Salaries 16,000	16,000	16,500	
Utilities 500	600	600	
2015 TOT 24,500	24,100	25,800	
2016 BUC 25,235	24,823	26,574	

formula bar (left): =C11*$C$3

formula bar (right) C11: =C6+C7+C8+C9+C10

B	January	February	March
INCREASE	1.03		
EXPENSES	January	February	March
Advertising	4600	4200	5200
Rent	2100	2100	2100
Supplies	1300	1200	1400
Salaries	16000	16000	16500
Utilities	500	600	600
2015 TOTAL	=C6+C7+C8+C	=D6+D7+D8+D9+	=E6+E7+E8+E9+E10
2016 BUDGET	=C11*$C$3	=D11*$C$3	=E11*$C$3

Figure 7.2

7.2.3 Tracing cell relationships

Two concepts are important to the understanding of cell relationships:

- **Cell precedents**: This is applicable only to cells that contain a formula, a formula cell's precedents are all the cells that contribute to the formulas results. A *direct precedent* is a cell that is used directly in the formula. An indirect precedent is a cell that isn't used directly in the formula but is used by a cell that is referenced in the formula

- **Cell dependents:** These formula cells dependents upon a particular cell. A cell's dependents consist of all formula cells that use the cell. Again, the formula cell can be a direct dependent or an indirect dependent.

For example, consider the formula entered in cell A4:

=SUM(A1:A3)

Cell A4 has three precedent cells (A1, A2, A3), which are all direct precedents. Cell A1, A2, and A3 all have at least one dependent cell (cell A4), and they are all direct dependents. If you are about to delete a formula, you may want to check if it has any dependents.

7.2.3.1 Identifying precedence

You can identify cells used by a formula in many ways:

- **Press F2**. The cells that are used directly by the formula are outlined in colour, and the colour corresponds to the cells reference in the formula. In addition, the formula cell displays the formula text instead of the result. Note that the formula cell must be selected before you press F2. This technique is limited to identifying cells on the same sheet as the formula, and works on one formula cell at a time

- **Choose Home** ⇒ **Editing** ⇒ **Find & Select** ⇒ **Go To Special.** Select the **Precedents** option and then select either **Direct Only** (for direct precedents only) or **All Levels** (direct and indirect precedents). Click OK. Excel selects the precedent cells for the formula. This technique is limited to identifying cells on the same sheet as the formula

- **Press Ctrl + [.** This selects all direct precedent cells on the active sheet. The formula cell must be selected first

- **Press Ctlr + Shift + {.** This selects all the precedent cells (direct and indirect) on the active sheet. The formula cell must be selected first

Choose **Formula** ⇒ **Formula Auditing** ⇒ **Trace Precedents**. Excel will draw arrows to the precedent cells. Choose **Formula** ⇒ **Formula Auditing** ⇒ **Remove Arrows** to hide the arrows

Figure 7.3 shows a worksheet with precedent arrows drawn to indicate the precedents for the formula in cell B18 and D18

	A	B	C	D	E
1			**Monthly Family Budget**		
2					
3		Total Projected Cost	Total Actual Cost	Total Difference	
4		$ 8,731.00	$ 4,437.18	$ (4,293.82)	
5					
6	**Housing**	**Projected Cost**	**Actual Cost**	**Difference**	
7	Mortgage	$ 1,000.00	$ 1,250.00	$ 250.00	
8	Student Housing Rent	$ 750.00	$ 550.00	$ (200.00)	
9	Phone	$ 62.00	$ 100.00	$ 38.00	
10	Electricity	$ 4.00	$ 125.00	$ 121.00	
11	Gas	$ 22.00	$ 35.00	$ 13.00	
12	Water and sewer	$ 8.00	$ 8.00	$ -	
13	Cable	$ 34.00	$ 39.00	$ 5.00	
14	Waste removal	$ 10.00	$ 10.00	$ -	
15	Maintenance or repair	$ 23.00	$ 45.00	$ 22.00	
16	Supplies	$ 100.00	$ 50.00	$ (50.00)	
17	Other	$ 150.00	$ 25.00	$ (125.00)	
18	Total	$ 2,163.00	$ 2,237.00	$ 74.00	
19					

Figure 7.3

7.2.3.2 Identifying dependents

There are many ways to identify formula cells that use particular cells

Choose **Home Editing Find & Select** ⇒ **Go To Special.** Select the **Dependents** option and then select either Direct Only or All Levels. Click OK. Excel selects the cells that depend upon the active cells. This technique is limited to cells on the active sheet only

- Press **Ctrl +].** This selects all direct dependent cells on the active sheet. The formula cell must be selected first

- **Press Ctlr + Shift +}.** This selects all the dependent cells (direct and indirect) on the active sheet. The formula cell must be selected first

Choose **Formula** ⇒ **Formula Auditing** ⇒ **Trace Dependents**. Excel will draw arrows to the dependent cells. Click the formula multiple times to see additional levels of dependents. Choose **Formula** ⇒ **Formula Auditing** ⇒ **Remove Arrows** to hide the arrows

7.2.4 Tracing errors values

An error in one cell is often the result of an error in a precedent cell. Activate the cell that contains the error value and then choose **Formula** ⇒ **Formula Auditing** ⇒ **Error Checking** ⇒ **Tracing Error**. Excel draws arrows to indicate the error source.

7.2.5 Fixing circular reference errors

Excel displays a warning message – *Circular Reference* – with the cell address, if a circular reference occurs. It also draws arrows on the worksheet to help figure out the problem. If you can't figure out the cause of the problem, choose **Formula Formula Auditing Error Checking Circular References**. This command displays a list of all cells that are involved in the circular references. Start by selecting the first cell listed and then work your way down the list until you figure out the problem.

7.2.6 Using the background error-checking features

Excel's automatic error-checking feature can be enabled and disabled from the **Excel Options** dialog box shown in Figure 7.4. In addition, you can use the check boxes in the **Error Checking Rules** section to specify which type of error to check.

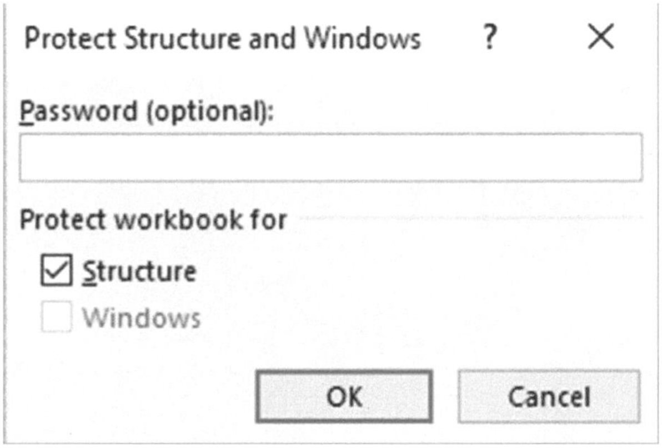

Figure 7.4

When error checking is turned on, Excel continually evaluate the formula in the worksheet. If an error is identified, Excel places a small triangle in the upper-left corner of the cell. When the cell is evaluated, a dropdown control appears. Clicking this dropdown control provides you with options. Figure 7.5 shows the option that appears when you click the dropdown control in a cell that contains the #DIV/0! Error. The options vary depending on the type of error.

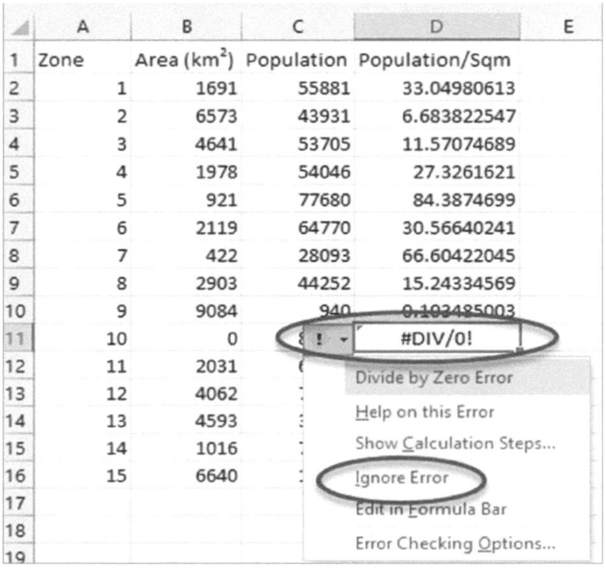

Figure 7.5

You can choose to ignore the error by pressing the **Ignore Error** option (Figure 7.5). This eliminates the cell from subsequent error checking. You can reset error checking for all previously ignored errors by using the "**Reset Ignored Errors**" button (see Figure 7.4)

7.2.7   Using the Formula Evaluator

Formula Evaluator lets you see the various parts of a nested formula evaluated in the order in which the formula is calculated. To use the formula evaluator:

- Select the cell that contains the formula

- Choose **Formula** ⇒ **Formula Auditing** ⇒ **Evaluate Formula** to display the **Evaluate Formula** dialog box (Figure 7.6)

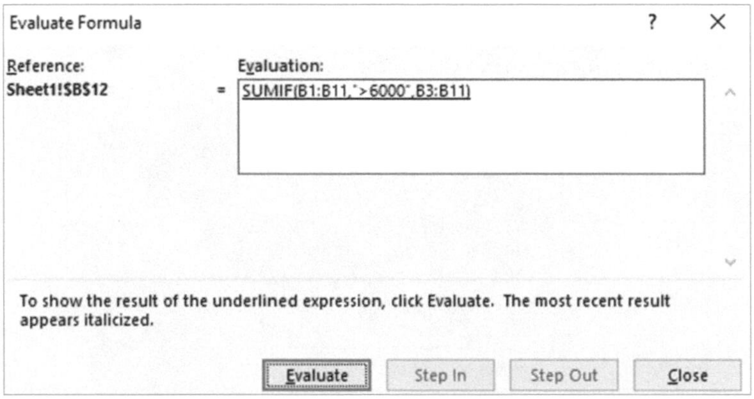

Figure 7.6

7.3   Using AutoCorrect

Auto correct is a feature that automatically correct common typing mistakes. You can also add words to the list that Excel correct automatically. The AutoCorrect dialog box appears in Figure 7.7

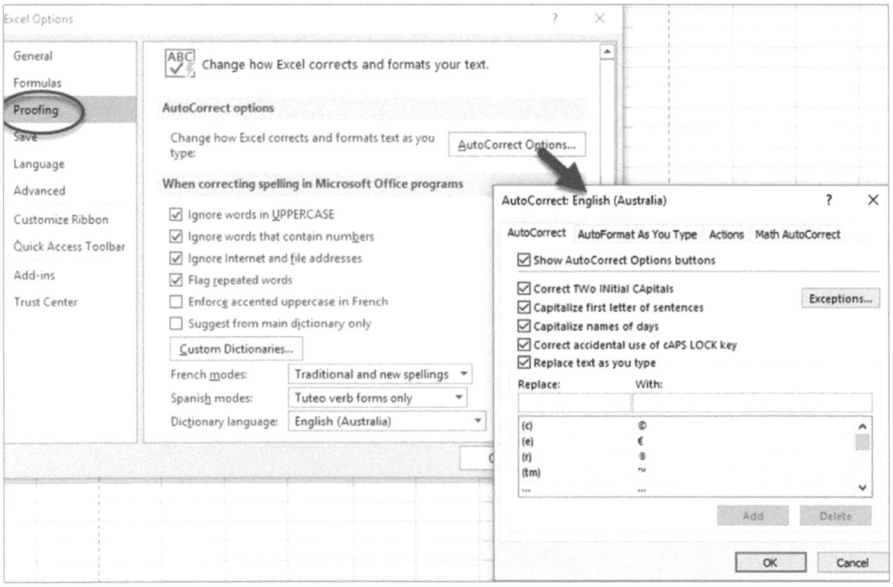

Figure 7.7

To access this feature, choose **File** ⇒ **Options**. In the Excel Options dialog box, select the **Proofing** tab and then click the **AutoCorrect Option** button. The dialog has several options (Figure 7.7) which are self-explanatory. You can add your own AutoCorrect entries. For example, if your company name is **GrandTotals Training & Consulting Pty Ltd**, you can shorten it to something like GTTC. Just enter GTTC in the **Replace** textbox in Figure 7.7 and in the **With** textbox enter the replacement text, in this example you would enter **GrandTotals Training & Consulting Pty Ltd.** Whenever you type GTTC in a cell, Excel will replace it with the full text.

8. Introducing Formulas and Functions

Formulas are used in Excel worksheets to calculate results from data stored in the worksheet or other worksheets. When data changes, the formula automatically recalculates the results with the new data. Excel formulas have the same general structure: an equal sign (=) followed by one or more *operands*, which can be values, cell references, ranges, range names, or function names, separated by one or more *operators*, which are symbols, such as a plus sign (+) that combine the operands.

8.1   Understanding Formula Basics

A formula can consist of any of these elements:

- Mathematical operators, such as +, *, >

- Cell references (including named cells and ranges)

- Values or text

- Worksheet functions (such as SUM or AVERAGE)

Here are a few examples of formulas:

- =140*9.8

- =A5   Returns the value in cell A5. No calculation is performed

- =A3+B7   Adds the value in cell A3 to the value in cell B7

- =Income – Expenses   Subtracts the value in a cell named *Expenses* from the value in

In a cell named Income

- =SUM(A1:A10)   Adds all the values in cells A1 through A10

- =A1=C14   Logical comparison

Note that every formula begins with the equal sign (=)

8.1.1   Using operators in formulas

Operators are symbols that indicate what mathematical operations are to be performed by the formula. Examples of operators are:

Operator	Name	Example	Results
&	Concatenation	="Parts –" & "23A"	Parts-23A
=	Logical comparison	=A1=A2	Returns TRUE if A1 = A2
<>	Logical comparison	A1<>A2	Returns TRUE if A1 <> A2

8.1.2   Understanding operator precedence in formulas

It is best to utilize parentheses to override the order of precedence of computations. Expressions within parentheses are always evaluated first. In the following formula, the expression within the parentheses is evaluated first and the results multiplied by the value in cell B4:

=(B2-B3)*B4.

If the parentheses is not applied and the formula is written as B2-B3*B4, Excel will first multiple the values in cell B3 and B4 (because multiplication (*) has a higher precedence that minus (-)) and then subtract the results from the value in cell B2. In other words the results of the same expression with and without the parentheses are going to be different.

The following two expressions would produce the same result:

((B2*C2)+(B3*C3)+(B4*C4))*B6 and *(B2*C2+B3*C3+B4*C4)*B6.*

However it is obvious that using the extra (inner) parenthesis makes the formula easier to understand.

8.1.3 Using functions in formulas

Excel Functions are named computations that can be plugged into your formulas to hide some computational complexities or provide calculations that would otherwise be impossible to perform with worksheet formulas alone:

The formula (A1+A2+A3+A4+A5+A6+A7+A8+A9+A10)/10 can be replaced with the Excel function AVERAGE(A1:A10). Neither is there any way to compute the maximum value within a range without resulting to using the MAX() function.

8.1.3.1 Function arguments

The information inside the function parentheses is the argument list. Functions may use:

- No arguments (e.g. the **NOW()** function, which returns the current date and time)
- One argument (e.g. **PROPER("grandtotals consulting")**)
- A fixed number of arguments (e.g. **VLOOKUP(lookup_value, table_array,col_index, [range])**
- An indeterminate number of arguments (e.g. **SUM(number1, number2,…)**
- Optional arguments **VLOOKUP(lookup_value, table_array,col_index, [range_lookup])**

An argument can consist of a cell reference, literal values, literal text strings, expressions, and even other functions **(SUM(SQRT(4),SQRT(9)).** Here the arguments to the **SUM** function are themselves functions (the Square Root function)

Function Examples

- The TEXT Function:

The Excel TEXT function converts a supplied numeric value into text, in a user-specified format.

The format of the function is:

=TEXT(value, "Format As String)

Where the function arguments are:

value	-	A numeric value that you want to be converted into text.
"Format As String"	-	A text string that defines the formatting that you want to be applied to the supplied value.

Example 1

The examples below show the Text function, used to apply different formatting types to various numeric values.

Formulas:			Results:		
	A	B		A	B
1	Value	Formatted Value	1	Value	Formatted Value
2	07/07/2015	=TEXT(A2, "dd/mm/yyyy")	2	07/07/2015	07/07/2015
3	42192	=TEXT(A3, "dd/mm/yyyy")	3	42192	07/07/2015
4	42192	=TEXT(A4, "mmm dd yyyy")	4	42192	Jul 07 2015
5	18:00	=TEXT(A5, "hh:mm")	5	18:00	18:00
6	0.75	=TEXT(A6, "hh:mm")	6	0.75	18:00
7	36.363636	=TEXT(A7, "0.00")	7	36.363636	36.36
8	0.5555	=TEXT(A8, "0.0%")	8	0.5555	55.6%
9	567.9	=TEXT(A9, "$#,##0.00")	9	567.9	$567.90
10	-5	=TEXT(A10, "+ $#,##0.00;- $#,##0.00;$0.00")	10	-5	- $5.00
11	5	=TEXT(A11, "+ $#,##0.00;- $#,##0.00;$0.00")	11	5	+ $5.00
			12	0	$0.00

Note that the results of the Text function, in column B of the spreadsheet above, are all text values, rather than numeric values.

- The IF Function

The Excel **IF** function tests a user-defined condition and returns one result if the condition is true, and another result if the condition is false.

The syntax of the function is :

IF(logical_test, value_if_true, value_if_false)

where the arguments are as follows:

logical_test	-	The user-defined condition that is to be tested and evaluated as either TRUE or FALSE

			The result that is to be returned from the function if the supplied logical_test evaluates to TRUE
value_if_true	-		The result that is to be returned from the function if the supplied logical_test evaluates to TRUE
value_if_false	-		The result that is to be returned from the function if the supplied logical_test evaluates to FALSE

Example

The following example shows the Excel **IF** function applied to two sets of numbers. In this example, the logical_test checks whether the corresponding value in column B is equal to 0, and the function returns :

The text string "div by zero" if the value in column B is equal to 0

or

The value in column A divided by the value in column B if the value in column B is not equal to zero

	A	B	C	D
1	5	4	=IF(B1=0, "div by zero", A1/B1)	- returns the value 1.25
2	5	0	=IF(B2=0, "div by zero", A2/B2)	- returns the text string "div by zero"

- The CHOOSE Function

The Choose function allows you to specify up to 254 choices right in the syntax of the function.

Syntax: CHOOSE(*index_num, value1, value2*, ...)

The CHOOSE function will choose a value from a list of values based on *index_num*

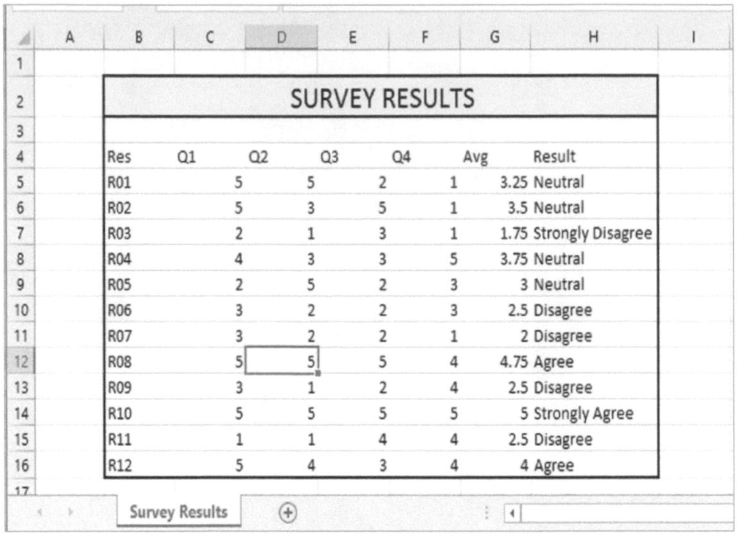

Res	Q1	Q2	Q3	Q4	Avg	Result
R01	5	5	2	1	3.25	Neutral
R02	5	3	5	1	3.5	Neutral
R03	2	1	3	1	1.75	Strongly Disagree
R04	4	3	3	5	3.75	Neutral
R05	2	5	2	3	3	Neutral
R06	3	2	2	3	2.5	Disagree
R07	3	2	2	1	2	Disagree
R08	5	5	5	4	4.75	Agree
R09	3	1	2	4	2.5	Disagree
R10	5	5	5	5	5	Strongly Agree
R11	1	1	4	4	2.5	Disagree
R12	5	4	3	4	4	Agree

Figure 8.1

The example in Figure 8.1 shows Survey data from many respondents. Columns B:F indicate their responses on five measures of a service. Column G calculates the average that ranges from 1 to 5. Say that you want to add descriptions to Column H to characterize the overall rating from the respondents. The following formula is used in cell H4:

=CHOOSE(G5,"Strongly Disagree", "Disagree", "Neutral", "Agree", "Strongly Agree")

- The INDIRECT Function

The Excel INDIRECT function converts a text string into a cell reference.

If you type the reference B1 in an Excel formula, Excel understands that this refers to cell B1. However, Excel does not understand the text string "B1" to be a reference. Therefore, if your cell reference takes the form of a text string, you will need to use the Indirect function to convert this into an actual cell reference.

The syntax of the Indirect function is:

INDIRECT(ref_text, [a1])

where the arguments are:

ref_text	-	The text describing the reference.
[a1]	-	An optional logical argument that defines the style of the ref_text reference. This can be either: • True - to denote that the reference is in A1 style • False - to denote that the reference is in R1C1 style If the [a1] argument is omitted, it takes on the default value "True".

By default, Excel uses the A1 referencing style. If you want to use the R1C1 referencing style, you will need to set this in your Excel options

Indirect Function Examples

The following spreadsheets show simple examples of the Excel Indirect function.

Formulas:

	A	B	C	D	E
1	=INDIRECT("C1")		8	9	0
2	=INDIRECT("D" & 4)		3	4	5
3	=INDIRECT("E" & ROW())		9	1	3
4	=SUM(INDIRECT("C4:E4"))		4	6	2

Results:

	A	B	C	D	E
1	8		8	9	0
2	6		3	4	5
3	3		9	1	3
4	12		4	6	2

8.2   Entering Formulas into Worksheet

Every formula must begin with an equal sign (=) to inform Excel that the cell contains a formula rather than text. Excel provides two ways to enter a formula into a cell: manually, or pointing to the cell references

8.2.1   Entering formulas manually

In a selected cell enter equal sign (=) followed by the formula. As you type, the characters appear in the cell and in the Formula bar. You can use the normal editing keys when entering a formula.

8.2.2   Entering formulas by pointing

This method allows you to provide a cell reference in the formula by pointing to a cell instead of typing the reference. For example, to enter the formula **=A1 + A2** in cell **A3**, follow these steps:

- Move the cell pointer to cell **A3**
- Type "=" to begin the formula. Notice that Excel displays Enter in the status bar
- Click cell **A1**
- Type a plus sign (+)
- Click cell **A2**
- Press Enter to signify the end of the formula

8.2.3   Pasting range names into formulas

If you create a formula based on a cell range and you later create a name for those cells that are used in the formula, Excel does not automatically replace the cell reference in the formula with the name. You have to manually replace the cell refence with the corresponding range name. For example if you have a formula in cell C11 as =SUM(C1:C10). If you later create a name such as "*TotalSales*" for the range C1:C10, Excel will not automatically replace the formula in cell C11 to read =SUM(TotalSales). If your formula uses named cells or ranges you can either type the name in place of the address, or choose the name from a list to insert into the formula. Two ways to insert a name into a formula:

- Select the name from a drop –down list as shown below:

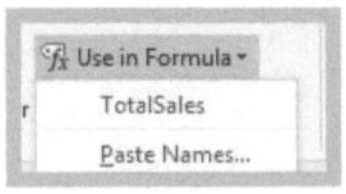

The **Use in Formula** option is accessed from the **Defined Names** group on the **Formula** tab

- • The other way to insert a name in a formula is by pressing F3. The **Paste Name** dialog box appears (Figure 8.2). Select the name from the list and press OK (or double-click the name). If no names are defined, pressing F3 has no effect.

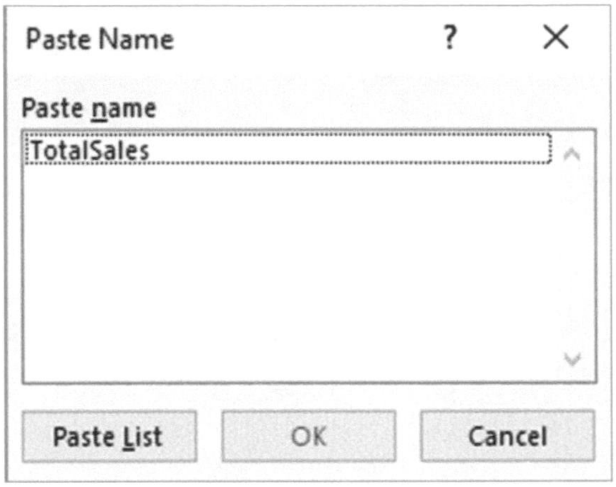

Figure 8.2

8.2.4 Tips for entering functions

One way to insert a function is to use tools in the Function Library group of the Formula tab (Figure 8.3).

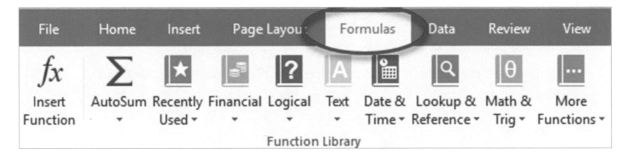

Figure 8.3

Click the function you want, and Excel displays its Function Argument dialog box where you provide the function's arguments.

Yet another way to insert a function into a formula is to use the **Insert Function** dialog box (Fig 8.4). Several ways are available to access the **Insert Function** dialog box:

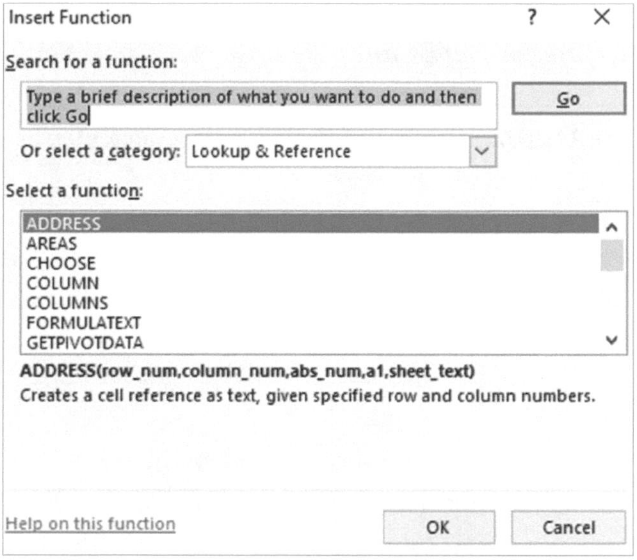

Figure 8.4

- Choose **Formula** ⇒ **Function Library** ⇒ **Insert Function**

- Use the Insert Function command, which appears at the bottom of each drop-down list in the **Formula** ⇒ **Function Library** group

- Click the **Insert Function** icon (displayed as *fx*), which is directly to the left of the Formula bar

- Press **Shift + F3**

> *Note: To be able to display the Insert Function dialog box (Figure 8.4), the formula cell must be empty. If the cell you have selected already contains a formula (such as SUMIF), the dialog box you receive will relate to that function.*

8.3 Using Cell References in Formulas

Most formulas in worksheets include references to cells or ranges. These references enable the formulas to work dynamically with the data contained in those cells or ranges.

8.3.1 Relative, absolute and mixed references

There are three types of references used in formulas:

- **Relative**: The row and column references can change when the formula is copied to another cell because the references are offset from the current row and column. This is the default in formulas.

- **Absolute:** The row and column references don't change when you copy the formula because the reference is to an actual cell address. An absolute reference uses two dollar signs in its address: one for the column letter and the one for the row letter (such as $A$5)

- **Mixed:** Either the row or column reference is relative, and the other is absolute. Only one of the address parts is absolute (for example $A4 or A$4)

> *Note: The type of reference used is important only if you plan to copy the formula to other cells*

Open C:\GrandTotal\Course Outline\GT002_Adv\cell references.xlsx and examined the formulas.

8.3.2 Changing the Types of References

You can manually enter the dollar sign ($) in your formulas manually, or you can use a shortcut: the F4 key. Pressing F4 repeatedly in the formula causes Excel to cycle through all the four reference types in a sequence such as A1 ⇒ $A$1 ⇒ A$1 ⇒ $A1

8.3.3 Referencing cells outside the worksheet

Formulas can also refer to cells in other worksheet (could be in other workbooks). Excel uses special notations to handle these types of references.

8.3.3.1 Cells in other worksheets

To use a reference to a cell in another worksheet in the same workbook, precede the cell address with the worksheet name, followed by an exclamation point such as **=A1*Sheet2!A1**. This formula multiplies the value in **A1** on the current worksheet with the value of **A1** on **Sheet2** in the same workbook.

8.3.3.2 Cells in other workbooks

To refer to a cell in a different workbook, use this format:

=[WorkbookName]SheetName!CellAddress

The following is an example of this format. It uses a cell reference in Sheet1 worksheet in a workbook named Budget:

=[Budget.xlsx]Sheet1!A1

A workbook name that includes spaces must be enclosed within single quotation marks:

=A1* '[Budget For 2015.xlsx]Sheet1'!A1

When a formula refers to a different workbook, the other workbook doesn't have to be open. If the workbook is closed, however, you must add the complete path to the reference. Such as:

='\\C:\GrandTotals\ Course Outline\GT002_Adv \[Budget.xlsx]Sheet1'!$D$7

Note: To create formulas that refers to cells in different worksheet, point to the cells rather than enter manually. Doing so allows Excel to take care of the details regarding the workbook and worksheet references. The workbook must be open

If you point to different worksheet or workbook when creating a formula, you'll notice that Excel always uses absolute cell references. Therefore, if you plan to copy the formula to other cells, make sure you change the cell references to relative before you copy.

8.4 Using Formulas in Tables

A table is a specially designated range of cells, set up with column headers. Formulas can also be used in the data in tables.

8.4.1 Summarizing data in tables

Month	Projected	Actual
Jan	4,000	3,255
Feb	4,000	4,102
Mar	4,000	3,982
Apr	5,000	4,598
May	5,000	5,873
Jun	5,000	4,783
Jul	5,000	5,109
Aug	6,000	5,982
Sep	6,000	6,201
Oct	7,000	6,833
Nov	8,000	7,983
Dec	9,000	9,821

Figure 8.5

Figure 8.5 shows a simple table with three columns. The data range was converted to a table by choosing **Insert ⇨ Tables ⇨ Table**.

To calculate the total projected and total actual sales, you don't even need to write a formula. Simply click a button to add a row of summary formula to the table:

1. Activate any cell in the table
2. Place a check mark next to **Table Tools ⇨ Design ⇨ Table Style Options ⇨ Total Row**
3. Activate a cell in **Total Row** and use the drop-down list to select the type of summary formula to use (Fig 8.6). For example, to calculate the sum of the Actual column, select SUM from the drop-down list in cell D15. Excel creates this formula:
   =SUBTOTAL(109, [Actual])

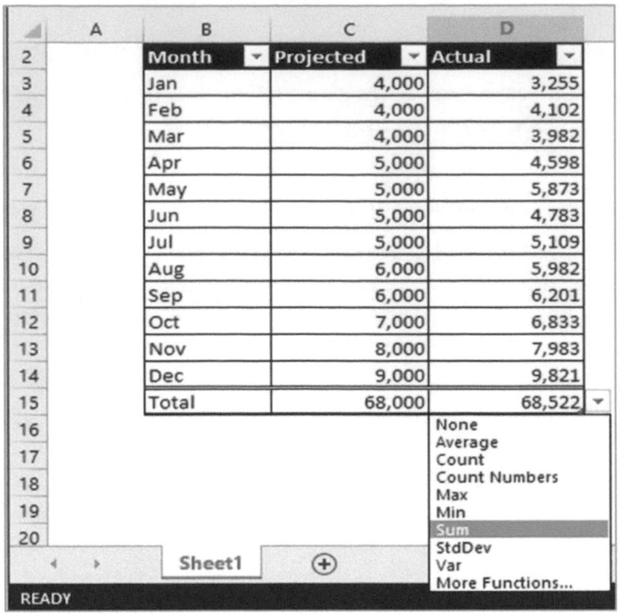

Month	Projected	Actual
Jan	4,000	3,255
Feb	4,000	4,102
Mar	4,000	3,982
Apr	5,000	4,598
May	5,000	5,873
Jun	5,000	4,783
Jul	5,000	5,109
Aug	6,000	5,982
Sep	6,000	6,201
Oct	7,000	6,833
Nov	8,000	7,983
Dec	9,000	9,821
Total	68,000	68,522

Figure 8.6

8.4.2 Using formulas within a table

You may use formulas within a table to perform calculations that use other columns in the table. For example, in the table shown in Figure 8.6, you may want a column that shows the difference between the **Actual** and **Projected** amount. To add this formula:

1. Activate cell E2 and type "**Difference**" for column header. Excel automatically expands the table to include the new column
2. In cell E3, type "="
3. Click D3, then type a minus sign (-)
4. Click C3
5. Press Enter to end the formula. Excel copies the formula to all rows in the table

The formula in the Difference column is: **=[@Actual]-[@Projected]**

> ***Note: The at symbol (@) that precede the column header represents "this row". So, [@Actual] means "the value in the 'Actual' column in this row"***
> ***Note: When you add a formula to a column in a table, Excel displays a Smart Tag. To override the automatic column formulas, click the Smart Tag and choose Stop Automatically Creating Columns. Use this option if you need a different formula for different rows within the table. See Figure 8.7***

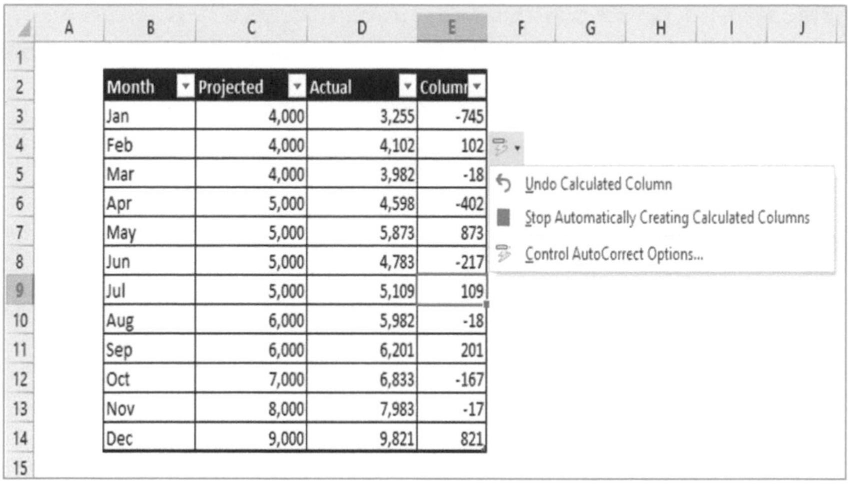

Month	Projected	Actual	Column
Jan	4,000	3,255	-745
Feb	4,000	4,102	102
Mar	4,000	3,982	-18
Apr	5,000	4,598	-402
May	5,000	5,873	873
Jun	5,000	4,783	-217
Jul	5,000	5,109	109
Aug	6,000	5,982	-18
Sep	6,000	6,201	201
Oct	7,000	6,833	-167
Nov	8,000	7,983	-17
Dec	9,000	9,821	821

Figure 8.7

8.4.3 Referencing data in a table

Excel offers some other ways to refer to data that's contained in a table by using the table name and column headers. For example, to calculate the sum of all the data in the table named Table1, use the following formula: = SUM(Table1). This formula returns the sum of all the data in the table (excluding calculated Total Row value, if any).

The following returns of the data in the Actual column: **SUM(Table1[Actual).** Note that if you precede the table name with the @ symbol, Excel will give you the row value that is adjacent to the row.

8.4.4 Specifying when formulas are calculated

You can control the timing of Excel calculations to be either Automatic (when a formula is entered or edited) or to manual:

Formula ➡ Calculations ➡ Calculation Options ➡ Manual

Advanced Naming Techniques

Range names makes it easier to understand and modify formulas. Dealing with meaningful names such as ***AnnualSales*** is much easier than dealing with a range reference, such as AB12:AB68

8.5 Using names for constants

It is possible to give a name in an item that even doesn't appear in a cell. For example, if you use a tax rate in spreadsheet formulas, you don't need to store the rate in a cell before you can use it.

To create a named constant:

1. **Choose Formula ➡ Defined Names ➡ Define Name.** The New Name dialog box appears. See Figure 8.8 below
2. Enter the name (for example, **TaxRate**) into the Name field and select a scope for the name
3. Click the **Refers To** text box, delete the contents, and enter a value. Such as **0.075** (for TaxRate) and click **OK** to close the dialog box.

You just created a name that refers to a constant (not stored in any cell). If you type **=TaxRate** into a cell, the formula returns 0.075 – the value for the named constant. You also can use the constant in a formula, such as **=A1*TaxRate**

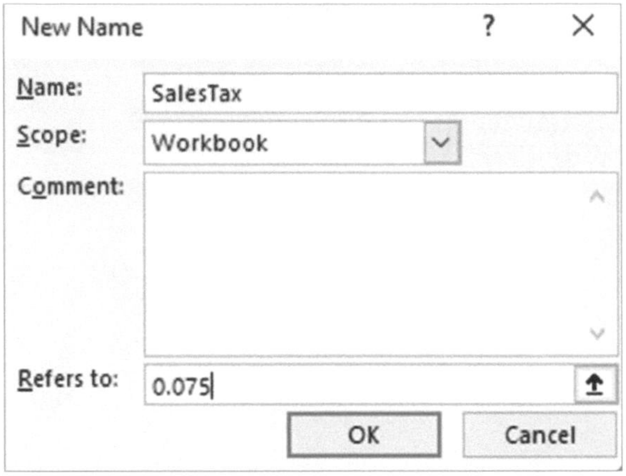

Figure 8.8

Note: If you change the name of a named constant, any formula that uses the name will be updated automatically to use the new name. A constant can also be text such as a company name

If you can't remember the name of a constant, you can select it from a drop-down list and paste into a formula as shown in Figure 8.9 below:

Figure 8.9

8.6 Using names for formulas

In addition to creating named constants, you can also create named formulas. Like named constants, named formulas don't appear in the worksheet. You create a named formula in the same way as named constants. When you use the pointing technique to create a formula in the **Referred To** field of the **New Name** dialog box, Excel always uses absolute cell references.

8.7 Using range intersection

Range intersection refers to individual cells that two ranges have in common. Excel uses the *intersection operator* – a space character – to determine the overlapping references in two ranges.

Figure 8.10 shows a simple example. The formula in cell B9 is

=A3:D3 B1:B6

The formula returns 643, the value in cell B3 – that is, the value at the intersection of the two ranges:

	A	B	C	D
1	204	639	956	754
2	563	190	783	834
3	783	643	894	863
4	902	894	723	903
5	745	463	890	342
6	675	837	638	382
7				
8				
9		643		
10				

Figure 8.10

You can use named cells to enhance the value of range intersection:

	A	B	C	D	E
1		Quarter1	Quarter2	Quarter3	Quarter4
2	North	204	639	956	754
3	South	563	190	783	834
4	East	783	643	894	863
5	West	902	894	723	903
6					

Figure 8.11

First you create names with row and column headers:

Select the entire table and then choose **Formula** ⇨ **Defined Names** ⇨ **Create from Selection** to create names automatically by using the top row and column headers. For example, one of the names created is **South** for the range B3:E3

With these names defined, you can create formulas that are easy to read and use. For example, to calculate the total for **South,** enter this formula:

=SUM(South)

To refer to a single cell, use the intersection operator:

=Quarter1 West

The formula returns the value for the first quarter for the West region (intersection of *Quarter1* and *West* ranges, i.e. 902 in Figure 8.11).

8.8   Applying names to existing references

When you create a name for a cell or a range, Excel doesn't automatically use the names in place of existing references in formulas. For example, if you have a formula such as =A1-A2 in cell F10. And later you define a name for cell A1 such as *Income* and *Expenses* for cell A2, the original formula does not automatically become *=Income-Expenses*.

To apply names to cell references in formulas:

- Select the range to be modified
- Choose **Formulas** ⇨ **Defined Names** ⇨ **Define Name** ⇨ **Apply Name**
- Select the name you want to apply and click OK. See Figure 8.12

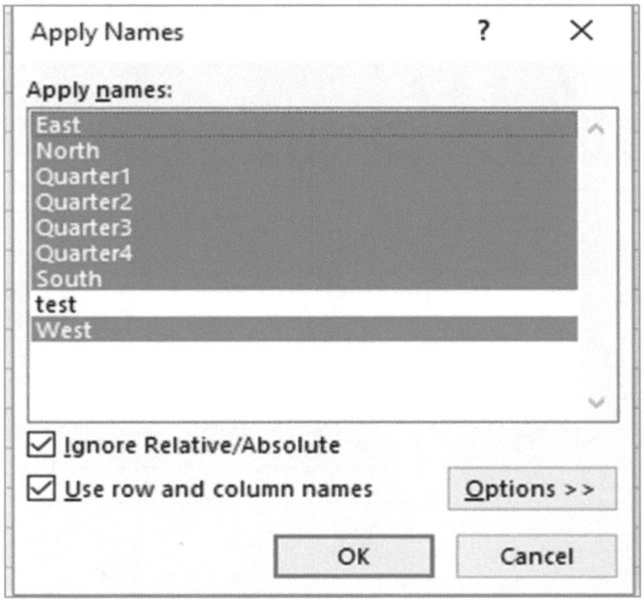

Figure 8.12

9. Text Manipulating Functions

Excel can use formulas to manipulate the text contained in cells. A cell entry that is considered by Excel not to be a formula or a number (date or time) default to a text.

9.1   Determining whether two strings are identical

To compare the contents of two cells you can use a formula such as:

=A1=A2.

If Cell A1 contains "january" and cell A2 contains "JANUARY" the formula returns TRUE. Thus the straight cell comparison formula above is not case sensitive. To compare a case sensitive comparison use the following formula:

=EXACT(A1,A2)

In the "January" case example, this formula will yield a "FALSE" result

9.2   Joining two or more cells

Excel uses the ampersand (&) as its concatenation (joining) operator. If cell A1 contains the text "**Code**" and cell A2 contains the text "**001**", the following formula will produce **"Code-001":**

=A1&"-"&A2

If you have a numbers in range A1:A10, for example, the following formula will combine a text with the result of an expression that returns the maximum value in the range:

"The largest value in the range is " & MAX(A1:A10). If the maximum value in range A1:A10 is 400, the expression will produce: **The largest value in the range is 400.**

9.3 Displaying formatted values as text

The **TEXT** function enables you to display a value in a specific number format. Figure 9.1 shows a simple worksheet. The formula in cell C5 is

="The net profit is " &B3

C5		▼	⋮	✕	✓	*fx*	="The net profit is " & TEXT(B3, "$#,##0")

◢	A	B	C	D	E	F	G	H
1	Gross	$477.53						
2	Expenses	$367,834						
3	Net	$109,699						
4								
5			The net profit is $109,699					

Figure 9.1

Here is a revised formula that uses the TEXT function to apply formatting to the value in cell B3

=**"The net profit is** " & TEXT(B3, "$#,##0"). The formula produces the following result:

The net profit is $109,699. The second argument of the TEXT function consists of standard Excel format string.

9.4 Displaying formatted currency values as text

The Excel **DOLLAR** function converts a number to text using the currency format. It takes two arguments: the number to convert and the number of decimal places to display. The following formula returns *Total: $1, 287.37* (the second argument for the DOLLAR function specifies the number of decimal places):

=Total: "&DOLLAR(1287.367, 2)

9.5 Removing excess spaces and nonprintable characters

When data is imported into Excel, they could contain excess spaces or some other (often unprintable) characters. There are two functions to help clean up such data:

- **TRIM** removes all leading and trailing spaces and replaces internal strings of multiple spaces with a single space
- **CLEAN** removes all nonprinting characters from a string

Example of the TRIM function:

TRIM(" GrandTotals Training and Consulting. ") returns:

GrandTotals Training and Consulting.

9.6 Counting characters in a string

Use the **LEN** function to return the number of characters in its single argument. If cell A1 contains the text "**September Sales**", the formula =LEN(A1) returns 15 (the number of characters in the text)

9.7 Changing the case of a text

Excel provides three functions to change the case of text:

- **UPPER**: Converts the text to ALL UPPERCASE

    Example: =UPPER("GrandTotals training & consulting")
    Result : GRANDTOTALS TRAINING & CONSULTING

- **LOWER**: Converts the text to all lowercase

    Example: =LOWER("GrandTotals TRAINING & Consulting")
    Result: grandtotals training and consulting

- **PROPER**: Converts the text to Proper Case

    Example: PROPER("GrandTotals training & consulting")

Result: Grandtotals Training & Consulting

9.8 Extracting characters from a string

Some useful Excel functions for extracting characters are:

- **LEFT**: Returns a specified number of characters from the beginning of a string
- **RIGHT**: Returns a specified number of characters from the end of a string
- **MID**: Returns a specified number of characters beginning at a specified position within a string.

The following formula returns the last ten characters from cell A1. If A1 contains fewer than ten characters, the formula returns all text in the cell:

=RIGHT(A1)

The next formula uses the MID function to return five characters from cell A1, beginning at character position 2, returning characters 2 through 6:

=MID(A1, 2, 5)

9.9 Replacing text with other text

The **SUBSTITUTE** function is used to replace part of a text string with some other text. Use this function when you know the character(s) to be replaced but not the position.

The **REPLACE** function replaces text that occurs in a specific location within a string. Use this function when you know the position of the text to be replaced but not the actual text.

Example: = SUBSTITUTE("2012 Budget", "2012", "2013"). This produces the text "**2013 Budget**"

Example: = REPLACE("Parts-554", 5, 1, "")

9.10 Finding and searching within a string

The **FIND** and **SEARCH** functions enable you to locate the starting position of a particular substring within a string:

- **FIND** finds a substring within another text and returns the starting position of the substring. Use this function for case-sensitive text comparison
- **SEARCH** finds a substring within another text and returns the starting position of the substring. Use this function for non-case-sensitive text comparison or when you need to use wildcard characters.

Example: **FIND**("t", "GrandTotals Training & Consulting"). Result is 8. This is case sensitive search, so finds "t" not "T"

You can use the REPLACE function in conjunction with the SEARCH function to replace part of a text with another string. In effect you use the SEARCH function to find the starting location used by the REPLACE function.

For example, assume that cell A1 contains the text *"Annual Profit Figures"*. The following formula searches for the six-letter word *"Profit"* and replaces it with the word *"Loss""*

    =REPLACE(A1, SEARCH("Profit", A1),6,"Loss")

The same outcome can be achieved with the SUBSTITUTE function:

SUBSTITUTE(A1, "Profit" "Loss")

Example: Extracting all but the first word of a string:

The following formula returns the contents of cell A1 except for the first word:

    =RIGHT(A1, LEN(A1) – FIND(" ", A1, 1))

10. Working with Dates and Times

To be able to work with dates and times, it is necessary to have a good understanding of how Excel handles time-based information.

10.1   How Excel Handles Dates and Times

To Excel, a date is simply a number. A date is a serial number that represents the number of days since the fictitious date of January 0, 1900. Thus, a serial number of 1 corresponds to January 1, 1900. A serial number of 2 corresponds to January 2, 1900, and so on. The serial number 42327 corresponds to November 19, 2015 when this manual was produced. In other words, there is approximately 42327 days between January 1, 1900 and November 19, 2015. This concept makes it easy to perform calculations based on dates. For example, finding the number of days between two days becomes just a matter of subtraction.

10.1.1   The time serial numbers

The serial number concept for dates in Excel can be extended to time. In other words, Excel works with time by using fractional days. For example, the date serial number for November 11, 2015 is 42327. Noon (halfway through the day) on this day is represented internally as 42327.5.

10.1.2   Entering times

As with entering dates, you normally don't have to worry about the actual time serial number.

Table 10.1 show examples of time format that Excel recognizes.

Table 10.1

Entry	Excel Interpretation
11:30 am	11:30 AM
11:30:00 AM	11:30 AM
11:30 pm	11:30 PM
11:30	11:30 AM
13:30	1:30 PM

If you want to enter a combination of date and time into Excel, do so by entering a recognised date format followed by a space, and then a recognised time entry format, such as: 11/10/2015 11:20

10.2   Working with Date-Related Worksheet Functions

Excel date functions are accessible by choosing **Formula** ➡ **Function Library** ➡ **Date & Time**

Below are some examples of Date-related functions:

Table 10.2

Function	Description
DATE	Returns the serial number of a particular date

DAY	Returns the day of the month
DAYS	Returns the number of days between two dates
EDATE	Returns the date that represents the indicated number of months before or after the start date
EOMONTH	Returns the last day of the month before or after a specified number of months
MONTH	Converts serial number to a month
NETWORKDAYS	Returns the number of work days between two dates
NETWORKDAYS.INTL	An international version of NETWORKDAYS function, which allows nonstandard weekend days
NOW	Returns the current date and time
TODAY	Returns today's date
WEEKDAY	Returns the day of the week
WORKDAY	Returns the date before or after a specified number of workdays
WORKDAY.INTL	An international version of WORKDAY, which allows non-standard weekend days
YEAR	Returns the year part of a date

10.2.1   Displaying the current date

The following formula uses the TODAY function to display the current date in a cell:

=TODAY()

You can also combine the date with text:

="**Today is** " &TEXT(TODAY(), "dddd, mmm d, yyyy")

10.2.2   Displaying any date

The DATE function can be used to enter a date into a cell. The syntax is DATE(year, month, day). Example: DATE(A2, B2, C2).

10.2.3   Converting a nondate string to a date

You may import data that contains date as coded string. For example, the following text represents November 19, 2015 (a four-digit year followed by a two-digit month, then a two-digit day):

20151119

You can use the following formula to convert the above coded date to actual date (assume A1 contains the code:

=DATE(LEFT(A1, 4), MID(A1, 5, 2), RIGHT(A1, 2))

10.2.4 Calculating the number of days between two dates

If cells A1 and B1 both contains dates, a simple subtraction gives the number of days between the two dates: A1-B1. To ignore negative number use ABS(B1-A1).

The DAYS() function is also available to compute the number of days between two dates:

DAYS(end_date, start_date)

10.2.5 Calculating the number of workdays between two dates

The NETWORKDAYS function returns the number of days between two days minus weekends (Saturday and Sundays) and holidays (usually stored in a range of cells).

Figure 40 shows a worksheet that calculates the workdays between two dates. The range A2:A11 contains a list of holiday dates. The two formulas in column C calculates the workdays between the dates in column A and column B. For example, the formula in cell C15 is

=NETWORKDAYS(A15, B15, A2:A11)

	A	B	C
1	Date	Holiday	
2	1/01/2013	New Year's Day	
3	21/01/2013	Queen's Birthday	
4	18/02/2013	ANZAC Day	
5	27/05/2013	Australia Day	
6	4/07/2013	Foundation Day	
7	2/09/2013	Labour Day	
8	14/10/2013	Boxing Day	
9	11/11/2013	Veterans Day	
10	28/11/2013	Good Friday	
11	25/12/2013	Christmas Day	
12			
13			
14	First Day	Last Day	Working Day
15	Tuesday 1/1/2013	Monday 1/7/2013	4
16	Tuesday 1/1/2013	Monday 12/31/2013	251

Figure 10.1

10.2.6 Offsetting a date using only workdays

The WORKDAY function is the opposite of the NETWORKDAYS function. For example, the following are the facts about a project:

Project Start Date: **January 4, 2015**

Ten *workdays* required to complete the project (workday: Monday – Friday)

Project Completion Date?

Project to complete on **=WORKDAY("1/4/2015",10)**

10.2.7   Determining the day of the week

The WEEKDAY function accepts a date argument and returns and integer between 1 and 7 that corresponds to the day of the week. The following formula returns the day of the week for today:

=WEEKDAY(Today()).

Optional second argument can be specified based on the information figure 10.2:

```
=WEEKDAY(DATE(2017,12,24),1

  WEEKDAY(serial_number, [return_type])  mbers 1 (Sunday) through 7 (Saturday)
                                   2 - Numbers 1 (Monday) through 7 (Sunday)
                                   3 - Numbers 0 (Monday) through 6 (Sunday)
                                  11 - Numbers 1 (Monday) through 7 (Sunday)
                                  12 - Numbers 1 (Tuesday) through 7 (Monday)
                                  13 - Numbers 1 (Wednesday) through 7 (Tuesday)
                                  14 - Numbers 1 (Thursday) through 7 (Wednesday)
                                  15 - Numbers 1 (Friday) through 7 (Thursday)
                                  16 - Numbers 1 (Saturday) through 7 (Friday)
                                  17 - Numbers 1 (Sunday) through 7 (Saturday)
```

Figure 10.2

If today is **Sunday, 24 December 2017**, and we accept Sunday as the first day of the week, the **WEEKDAY** function can be entered in three ways:

- =WEEKDAY(TODAY()),1)
- =WEEKDAY(DATE(2017, 12, 24),1)
- =WEEKDAY("24/12/2017",1)

10.2.8   Determining a day's quarter

For financial reports, it is usually useful to present information in terms of quarters. The following formula returns an integer between 1 and 4 that corresponds to the calendar quarter for the date in cell A1:

=ROUNDUP(MONTH(A1)/3, 0)

The formula divides the month number by 3 and then rounds up the result

10.3   Working with Time-Related Worksheet Functions

The table below summarizes the time-related functions available in Excel. These functions work with date serial numbers.

Table 10.3 Time related function

Function	Description
HOUR	Returns the hour part of a serial number
MINUTE	Returns the minute part of a serial number

Function	Description
NOW	Returns the current date and time
SECOND	Returns the second part of a serial number
TIME	Returns the serial number of a specified time
TIMEVALUE	Converts time as text to a serial number

10.3.1 Displaying the current time

To display the current time:

=NOW()-TODAY()

You need to format the cell with a time format. Choose **Home Format Number** and select *Time* from the drop-down list. Or simply use the NOW function and apply a format that shows the time only.

10.3.2 Displaying any time

You can enter time in a cell making sure to include at least one colon (:), for example, 10:30:12.

You can also use the TIME function. For example: =TIME(A1, B1, C1), where cells A1, B1, C1 corresponds to the hour, minute and seconds respectively.

10.3.3 Calculating the difference between two times

To find the difference between two times, just subtract the two dates.

	A	B	C	D
1	Shift Start	Shift End	Formula	Hours Worked
2	8:00 AM	5:30 PM	=B2-A2	9:30
3	10:00 AM	6:00 AM	=B3-A3	##############
4	9:00 AM	4:30 PM	=B4-A4	7:30
5	11:30 AM	7:45 PM	=B5-A5	8:15
6	6:15 AM	11:00 AM	=B6-A6	4:45

Figure 10.3

In figure 10.3 above, the hours worked are calculated by subtracting the start time from the finish time. Because in row 3 the shift spans midnight, a negative hour worked resulted in the calculation. The problem is indicated by the # symbol filing the cell. The following formula solves the negative hours worked problem:

IF(B2<A2, B2+1, B2) –A2

10.3.4 Working with non-time-of-day values

Some time values really do not represent actual time. For example, the time to complete a test (such as 00:45:00) does not represent the time of day. When such values are entered into a cell, Excel interprets it as 12:45:00, which works fine. Just format the cell appropriately. When such a number does not include an hour component, you must include at least one zero for the hour component. In the above example, if the zero for the missing hour is not included, Excel interprets the entry as 45 hours and 0 minutes.

11.   Creating Formulas That Counts and Sum

This section looks at some examples of counting and summing values in cells.

11.1   Counting and Summing Worksheet Cells

Generally, a *counting formula* returns the number of cells in a specified range that meet certain criteria. A *summing formula* returns the sum of the values of the cells in a range that meet certain criteria.

Table 11.1 shows Excel's common counting and summing functions

Table 11.1

Function	Description
COUNT	Returns the number of cells that contains a numeric value
COUNTA	Returns the number of nonblank cells
COUNTBLANK	Returns the number of blank cells
COUNTIF	Returns the number of cells that meet a specified criterion
COUNTIFS	Returns the number of cells that meet multiple criteria
DCOUNT	Counts the number of records that meet specified criteria; used with a worksheet database
DCOUNTA	Counts the number of nonblank records that meet specified criteria; used with a worksheet database
DSUM	Counts the sum of column that meet specified criteria; used with a worksheet database
SUBTOTAL	When used with a first argument of 2, 3, 102, or 103, returns a count of cells that comprise a subtotal; when used with a first argument of 9 or 109, returns the sum of cells that comprise a subtotal
SUM	Returns the sum of its arguments
SUMIF	Returns the sum of cells that meet a specified criterion
SUMIFS	Returns the sum of cells that meet multiple criteria
SUMPRODUCT	Multiplies corresponding cells in two or more ranges and returns the sum of those products

11.2   Basic Counting Formulas

Figure 11.1 shows a worksheet that uses formula (in column E) to summarize the contents of range A1:B10 named Data

	A	B	C	D	E	F
1	Jan	Feb		Total cells:	=ROWS(data)*COLUMNS(data)	20
2	525	718		Blank cells:	=COUNTBLANK(data)	6
3				Nonblank cells:	=COUNTA(data)	14
4	3			Numeric values:	=COUNT(data)	7
5	552	911		Non-text cells:	=SUM(IF(ISNONTEXT(data),1))	17
6	250	98		Text cells:	=SUM(IF(ISTEXT(data),1))	3
7				Logical values:	=SUM(IF(ISLOGICAL(data),1))	2
8	TRUE	FALSE		Error values:	=SUM(IF(ISERROR(data),1))	2
9		#DIV/0!		#N/A errors:	=COUNTIF(data,"#NULL")	0
10	Total	#NAME?		#NULL! Errors:	=COUNTIF(data,"#N/A")	0
11				#DIV/0! Errors:	=COUNTIF(data,"#DIV/0!")	1
12				#VALUE! Errors:	=COUNTIF(data,"#DIV/0!")	1
13				#REF! errors:	=COUNTIF(data,"#DIV/0!")	1
14				#NAME? errors:	=COUNTIF(data,"#NUM!")	0

Figure 11.1 Excel counting formulas

11.2.1   Counting the total number of cells

To count the total number of cells, multiply the number of columns by the number of rows:

=ROWS(Data) * COLUMNS(Data)

11.2.2   Counting blank cells

The following formula returns the number of blank (empty) cells in a range named Data:

=COUNTBLANK(Data)

The function also counts cells containing a formulas that returns empty string.

11.2.3   Counting non-blank cells

To count nonblank cells, use the *COUNTA* function:

=COUNTA(Data)

The COUNTA function Counts cells that contains values, text, or logical values (TRUE or FALSE)

11.2.4   Counting numeric cells

To count only the numeric cells in a range, use the following formula:

=COUNT(Data)

Dates and times are considered to be numeric.

11.2.5   Counting text cells

To count text cells, use array formula:

{=SUM(IF(ISTEXT(Data), 1))}

11.2.6   Counting non-text cells

Blank cells are also counted.

{=SUM(IF(ISNONTEXT(Data), 1))}

11.2.7   Counting logical values

{=SUM(IF(ISLOGICAL(Data), 1))}

11.2.8   Counting error values in a range

- ISERROR: Returns TRUE if cell contains any type of error value (#N/A, #VALUE!, #REF!, #DIV/0!, #NUM!, #NAME?, or #NULL!)
- ISERR: Returns TRUE if the cell contains any error value except #N/A
- ISNA: Returns TRUE if the cell contains the #N/A error value

The following example uses an array formula to return the total number of error cells in a range named Data:

{=SUM(IF(ISERROR(Data), 1))}

If you want to count specific types of errors, you can use the COUNTIF function. The following formula, for example, return the number of #DIV/0! Error values in the range named Data:

=COUNTIF(Data, "#DIV/0!")

11.3   Advanced Counting Formulas

The advanced counting techniques are based on more complex criteria.

11.3.1   Using the COUNTIF function

The COUNTIF function takes two arguments:

- **Range**: The range that contains the values that determine whether to include a particular cell in the range
- **Criteria**: The logical criteria that determine whether to include a particular cell in the count

=COUNTIF(Data, 12)	Returns the number of cells containing the value 12
=COUNTIF(Data, "<0")	Returns the number of cells containing a negative value
=COUNTIF(Data, "<>0")	Returns the number of cells containing values other than 0
=COUNTIF(Data, ">5")	Returns the number of cells containing values greater than 5
=COUNTIF(Data, A1)	Returns the number of cells containing values equal to the value in A1

=COUNTIF(Data, ">"&A1)	Returns the number of cells containing values greater than value in A1
=COUNTIF(Data, "*")	Returns the number of cells containing a text
=COUNTIF (Data, "???")	Returns the number of text cells containing exactly three characters
=COUNTIF(Data, "budget")	Returns the number of cells containing the single word budget (not case sensitive)
=COUNTIF(Data, "*budget*")	Returns the number of cells containing the text *budget* anywhere within the text
=COUNTIF(Data, "A*")	Returns the number of cells containing text that begins with the letter A (not case sensitive)
=COUNTIF(Data, TODAY())	Returns the number of cells containing the current data
=COUNTIF(Data, ">"&AVERAGE(Data)))	Returns the number of cells with a value greater than the range average
=COUNTIF(Data, "N/A")	Returns the number of cells containing the #N/A error value

Table 4

11.3.2   Counting cells based on multiple criteria

Figure 11.2 shows a sales data categorized by Month, Sales Rep, and Type. The worksheet contains four named ranges that correspond to the labels in row 1. The examples below use Figure 11.2 for reference.

	A	B	C	D
1	Month	SalesRep	Type	Amount
2	January	Albert	New	85
3	January	Albert	New	675
4	January	Sam	New	130
5	January	Caleb	New	1350
6	January	Caleb	Existing	685
7	January	Sam	New	1350
8	January	Caleb	New	475
9	January	Sam	New	1250
10	February	Sam	Existing	450
11	February	Albert	New	495
12	February	Caleb	New	210
13	February	Caleb	Existing	1050
14	February	Albert	New	140
15	February	Sam	New	900
16	February	Sam	New	900
17	February	Caleb	New	95
18	February	Caleb	New	780
19	March	Sam	New	900
20	March	Albert	New	875
21	March	Sam	New	50
22	March	Sam	New	875
23	March	Caleb	Existing	225
24	March	Caleb	New	225
25	March	Sam	Existing	175
26	March	Albert	New	400
27	March	Caleb	New	840

Figure 11.2: multiple criteria counting

11.3.2.1 Using the "And" criteria

The **AND** criteria count cells if all specified criteria are met. For example, count the number of cells where that Amount is greater than 100 and less than or equal to 200:

=COUNTIFS(Amount, ">100", Amount, "<=200")

Notice that even though this formula uses the And criteria the word "**AND**" does not appear in the formula.

Sometimes, the counting criteria will be based on cells other than the cells being counted. For example, to count the number of sales that meet the following criteria:

- Month is January and
- SalesRep is Sam and
- Amount is greater than 1,000:

Use the following formula:

=COUNTIFS(Month, "January",SalesRep, "Sam", Amount, ">1000")

11.3.2.2   Using the OR criteria

The **OR** criteria counts cells if any of the multiple conditions is met. The **OR** criteria can be achieved by using multiple COUNTIF functions. For example, to count the number of sales in January or February:

=COUNTIF(Month, "January") + CONTIF(Month, "February")

You can also use the COUNTIF function in an array formula. The following array formula, for example returns the same result as the previous formula:

{=SUM(COUNTIF(Month, {"January", "February"}))}

But if you base your Or criteria on cells other than the cells being counted, the COUNTIF function won't work. Suppose that you want to count the number of sales that meet at least one of the following criteria:

- Month is January or
- SalesRep is Sam or
- Amount is greater than 1,000

If you attempt to create a formula that uses COUNTIF, some double counting may occur. The solution is to use an array formula:

{=SUM(IF(Month="January") + (SalesRep = "Sam") + (Amount>1000),1))}

11.3.2.3   Combining And and Or criteria

In some cases, it may be necessary to combine the AND criteria and the OR criteria when counting. For example, you may want to count sales that meet both the following criteria:

- Month is January
- SalesRep is Sam or SalesRep is Caleb

The following array formula returns the number of sales that meet the criteria:

{=SUM(IF((Month="January") * ((SalesRep="Sam") + (SalesRep="Caleb")),1))}

11.3.2.4   Conditional Sums Using a Single Criterion

With conditional sum, values in a range that meet one or more conditions are included in the sum. The SUMIF function is for a single-criteria sum formulas. The SUMIF function takes three arguments:

- *Range*: The range containing the values that determine whether to include a particular cell in the sum
- *criteria*: An expression that determines whether to include a particular cell in the sum
- *sum_range*: Optional. The range that contains the cells to be summed. If omitted, the function uses the range specified in the first argument

The following examples are based on Figure 45, set up to track invoices

	A	B	C	D	E	F
1	InvoiceNum	Office	Amount	DateDue	Today	Difference
2	AG-0145	Perth	$5,000.00	1/04/2017	5/05/2017	-34
3	AG-0189	Sydney	$450.00	19/04/2017	5/05/2017	-16
4	AG-0220	Brisbane	$3,211.56	28/04/2017	5/05/2017	-7
5	AG-0310	Perth	$250.00	30/04/2017	5/05/2017	-5
6	AG-0355	Brisbane	$125.50	4/05/2017	5/05/2017	-1
7	AG-0409	Brisbane	$3,000.00	10/05/2017	5/05/2017	5
8	AG-0581	Perth	$2,100.00	24/05/2017	5/05/2017	19
9	AG-0600	Perth	$335.39	24/05/2017	5/05/2017	19
10	AG-0602	Brisbane	$65.00	28/05/2017	5/05/2017	23
11	AG-0633	Sydney	$250.00	31/05/2017	5/05/2017	26
12	Total		$14,787.45			29

Figure 11.3: conditional sum.xlsx

The worksheet (Fig 11.3) uses named ranges that correspond to the labels in row 1

11.3.2.5   Summing only negative values

=SUMIF(Difference, "<0")

Because the third argument was omitted (sum_range), the second argument ("<0") applies to the values in the Difference range.

11.3.2.6   Summing values based on a different range

Example:

=SUMIF(Difference, "<0", Amount)

11.3.2.7   Summing values based on a text comparison

Examples:

=SUMIF(Office, "=Perth", Amount)

=SUMIF(Office, "<>Perth", Amount)

11.3.2.8   Summing values based on a date comparison

Examples:

=SUMIF(DateDue, ">="&DATE(2013, 5, 1), Amount)

=SUMIF(DueDate, ">="&TODAY(), Amount)

12. Getting to Know the LOOKUP Formulas

This section discusses various techniques that can be employed to look up a value in a range of data. Excel has three worksheet functions (LOOKUP, VLOOKUP, and HLOOKUP) designed for this task.

12.1 Introducing Lookup Formulas

A lookup formula returns a value from a table by looking up another related value. Figure 47 uses four lookup formulas. The data range, C6:G14 is named **EmpData**. When you enter a last name in cell C2, lookup formulas in D2:G2 retrieve the marching information from the table. If the last name does not appear in Column C, the formula returns #N/A

◢	A	B	C	D	E	F	G
1			Last Name	First Name	Department	Extension	Date Hired
2	Enter a name -->		Sam	Tutu	Administration	1231	12/03/2011
3							
4							
5			Last Name	First Name	Department	Extension	Date Hired
6			Allen	Peters	Sales	4466	5/03/1998
7			Baker	Nanny	Operations	3432	16/04/2003
8			Bunnel	Kenneth	Marketing	4422	1/12/2010
9			Charles	Harry	Administraton	2822	16/09/1999
10			Sam	Tutu	Administraton	1231	12/03/2011
11			Davis	Rose	Administraton	2604	15/04/2017
12			Dunwell	John	Operations	3983	24/03/2017
13			Ellis	Paulina	Data Processing	2144	12/11/2017
14			Endow	Edwin	Data Processing	1102	13/09/2017

The following lookup formulas use the VLOOKUP functions:

D2=VLOOKUP(C2, EmpData, 2, FALSE)

E2=VLOOKUP(C2, EmpData, 3, FALSE)

F2=VLOOKUP(C2, EmpData, 4, FALSE)

G2=VLOOKUP(C2, EmpData, 5, FALSE)

12.2 Functions for Lookups

Table 12.1 Lookup functions

Function	Description
CHOOSE	Returns a specific value from a list of values supplied as arguments
HLOOKUP	Horizontal lookup. Searches for a value in the top row of a table and returns a value in the same column from a row you specify in the table
IF	Returns one value if a condition you specify is TRUE, and returns another if the condition is FALSE

Function	Description
IFERROR	If the first argument returns an error, the second argument is evaluated and returned. Otherwise the first argument is evaluated and returned
INDEX	Returns a value (or the reference to a value) from within a table or range
LOOKUP	Returns a value either from a one-row or one-column range. Another form of the LOOKUP function works like VLOOKUP but is restricted to returning a value from the last column of a range
MATCH	Returns a relative position of an item in a range that matches a specified value
OFFSET	Returns a reference to a range that is a specified number of rows and columns from a cell or range of cells
VLOOKUP	Vertical lookup. Searches for a value in the first column of a table and returns a value in the same row from a column you specify in the table

12.3 Basic Lookup Formulas

Excel provides three basic lookup functions: HLOOKUP, VLOOKUP, and LOOKUP. Also, the MATCH and INDEX functions are often used together in a single formula to return lookup values.

12.3.1 The VLOOKUP Function

The VLOOKUP function looks up a value in the *first* column of the lookup table and returns a corresponding value in a specified table column within the lookup table.

Syntax:

VLOOKUP(*lookup_value, table_array, col_index_num, range_lookup*)

If *range_lookup* is TRUE or omitted, an approximate match is returned. (If an exact match is not found, the next largest value that is less than lookup_value is returned). If FALSE, VLOOKUP will search for an exact match. If VLOOKUP can't find an exact match, the function returns #N/A.

Note: If the range_lookup value is TRUE, or omitted, the first column of the lookup table must be in ascending order.

*If lookup_value argument is text, and the range_lookup argument is FALSE, the lookup_value can include wildcard characters * and ?*

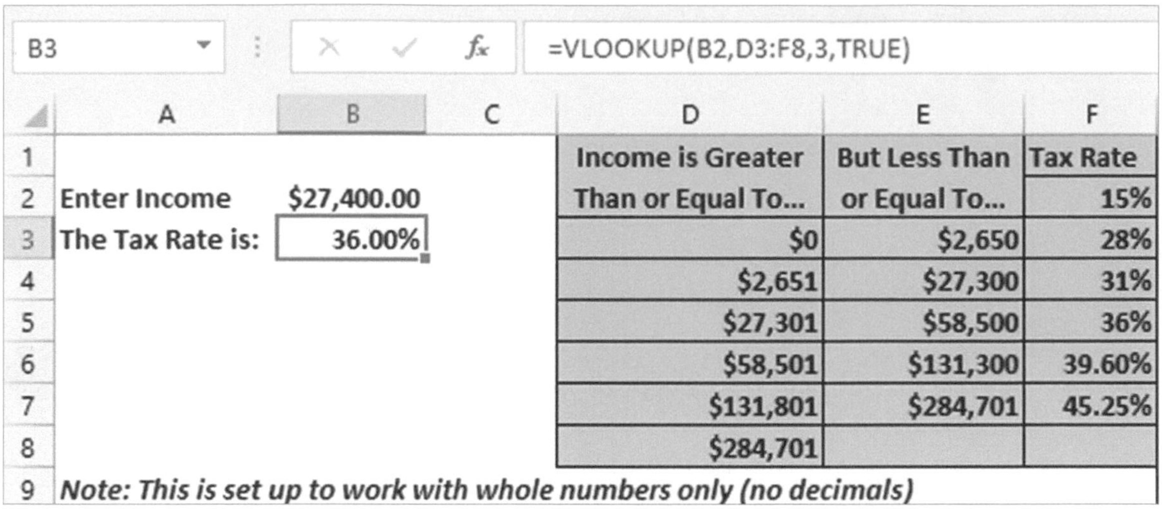

B3 =VLOOKUP(B2,D3:F8,3,TRUE)

	A	B	C	D	E	F
1				Income is Greater	But Less Than	Tax Rate
2	Enter Income	$27,400.00		Than or Equal To...	or Equal To...	15%
3	The Tax Rate is:	36.00%		$0	$2,650	28%
4				$2,651	$27,300	31%
5				$27,301	$58,500	36%
6				$58,501	$131,300	39.60%
7				$131,801	$284,701	45.25%
8				$284,701		
9	*Note: This is set up to work with whole numbers only (no decimals)*					

Figure 12.1: VLookupExample.xlsx

12.3.2 The HLOOKUP Function

Syntax:

HLOOKUP(lookup_value, table_array, row_index_num, range_lookup)

Note: If the lookup_value argument is text and the range_lookup argument is FALSE, the lookup_value can include wildcard characters * and ?

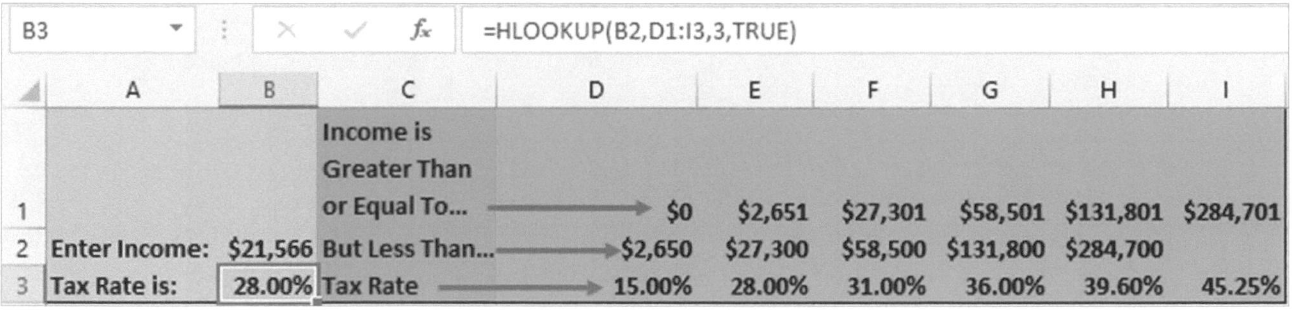

B3 =HLOOKUP(B2,D1:I3,3,TRUE)

	A	B	C	D	E	F	G	H	I
1			Income is Greater Than or Equal To... →	$0	$2,651	$27,301	$58,501	$131,801	$284,701
2	Enter Income:	$21,566	But Less Than... →	$2,650	$27,300	$58,500	$131,800	$284,700	
3	Tax Rate is:	28.00%	Tax Rate →	15.00%	28.00%	31.00%	36.00%	39.60%	45.25%

Figure 12.2: hlookupexample.xlsx

The formula in cell B3 (The Tax Rate) is

=HLOOKUP(B2,D1:I3,3,TRUE)

12.3.3 The LOOKUP function

The LOOKUP function looks in a one-row or one-column range (*lookup_vector*) for a value (*lookup_value*) and returns a value from the same position in a second one-row or one-column range (*result_vector*)

Syntax:

LOOKUP(*lookup_value, lookup_vector, result_vector*)

Values in *lookup_vector* must be in ascending order.

	Income is Greater Than or Equal To...	But Less Than	Tax Rate
Enter Income: $123,409 **The Tax Rate is:** 36.00%	$0	$2,650	15.00%
	$2,651	$27,300	28.00%
	$27,301	$58,500	31.00%
	$58,501	$131,800	36.00%
	$131,801	$284,700	39.60%
	$284,701		45.25%

Figure 12.3: lookupexample.xlsx

The formula in cell B3 is

=LOOKUP(B2, D2:D7, F2:F7)

12.3.4   Combining the MATCH and INDEX functions

The **MATCH** and **INDEX** functions are often used together to perform lookups. The MATCH function returns the relative position of a cell that matches a specified value.

The syntax for MATCH is:

MATCH(*lookup_value, lookup_array, match_type*)

> match_type = {-1, 0, 1 (default)}   (default):   MATCH finds the largest value less than or equal to *lookup_value*. Lookup_array must be in ascending order

> match_type = 0:   MATCH must find the value exactly equal to *lookup_value*

> match_type = -1:   MATCH finds the smallest value greater than or equal to lookup_value (*lookup_array* must be in descending order)

The syntax for INDEX is:

INDEX(*array, row_num, column_num*)

The idea of combining the MATCH and INDEX functions in a single formula is that you use *MATCH()* to get the *row_num* or *column_num* and then use *INDEX()* to return the required value.

	A	B	C	D	E
1					
2	Enter Account Number:	10-0009		Account Number	Account Name
3	Account Name is:	Brimson Furniture		10-0009	Brimson Furniture
4				02-0200	Chimera Illusions
5				01-0045	Door Stoppers Ltd
6				08-2255	Emiy's Sports Palace
7				12-1212	Katy's aper Products
8				12-3456	Meaghan Manufacturing
9				09-2111	O'Donoghue Inc.
10				14-1882	Real Solemn Officials
11				14-5741	Refco Office Solutions
12				07-0025	Renaud & Son
13				07-4441	Rooter Office Solvent
14				16-6658	Simpson's Ltd.
15				14-1882	Voyatzis Designs

Figure 12.4: Match_Index.xlsx

The formula in cell B4 uses the MATCH function to find the row number for Account Number *10-0009* (in cell B2) within the range D3:D15. It then uses the INDEX function to find the Account Name (within the range E3:E15) at the row number retrieved by the MATCH function:

=INDEX(E3:E15, MATCH(B2, D3:D15, 0), 2)

12.4 Specialized Lookup Formulas (Exercise)

12.4.1 Looking up an exact value

- Use the Exact Values.xlsx:

- Use the MATCH and INDEX functions to find the employee whose Employee Number is **1643**.

- Use the MATCH and INDEX functions to find the Employee Number for Linda Harper.

	A	B	C	D	E
1				Employee No	Employee Name
2	Employee No:	972		873	Charles Barkley
3	Employee Name:	Sally Rice		1109	Francis Jenikins
4				1549	James Brackman
5				1334	Linda Harper
6				1643	Louise Victor
7				1101	Melinda Hindquest
8				1873	Michael Orienthal
9				983	Peter Yates
10				972	Sally Rice
11				1398	Walter Granklin

Figure 12.5: Exact Value.xlsx

12.4.2 Looking up a value from multiple lookup tables

If you have more than one lookup table in a worksheet, you can use the IF function to determine which of the tables to use in a particular situation.

	A	B	C	D	E	F	G	H	I	J	K
1	Sales Reps	Years	Sales	Comm Rate	Cmmission		<3 Years Tenure			3+ Years Tenure	
2	Benson	2	$120,000	7.00%	$84,000		Amt Sold	Rate		Amt Sold	Rate
3	Davidson	1	$210,921	7.00%	$14,764		$0	1.50%		0	2.00%
4	Ellison	1	$100,000	7.00%	$7,000		$5,000	3.25%		50000	6.25%
5	Gomez	2	$87,401	6.00%	$5,244		$10,000	3.50%		100000	7.25%
6	Hernandez	6	$310,983	9.25%	$28,766		$20,000	5.00%		200000	8.25%
7	Kelly	3	$43,902	2.00%	$878		$50,000	6.00%		300000	9.25%
8	Martin	3	$121,021	7.00%	$8,471		$100,000	7.00%		500000	10.00%
9	Oswald	2	$908	2.00%	$18		$250,000	8.00%			
10	Reginald	1	$0	1.50%	$0						
11	Veras	4	$359,832	9.25%	$33,284						
12	Wilmington	4	$502,983	10.00%	$50,298						

Figure 12.6: multiple tables.xlsx

Figure 12.5 shows a workbook that calculates sales commission and contains two lookup tables: G3:H9 (named **CommTable1**) and J3:K8 (named **CommTable2**). The commission rate for a particular sales representative depends on the factors: The Sales Rep's years of service (column B) and the amount of the sales (column C). Column D contains formulas that look up the commission rate from the appropriate table. For example, the formula in cell D2 is

=VLOOKUP (C2, IF(B2<3, Commtable1, CommTable2), 2)

The second argument for the VLOOKUP function consists of an IF formula that uses the value in column B to determine which lookup table to use.

The formula in column E simply multiplies the sales amount in column C by the commission rate in column D. The formula in cell E2, for example, is

=C2*D2

13. Introducing Array Functions

Array formulas are probably the least understood and utilized features of Excel.

An *array* is a group of cells or values that Excel treats as a unit. In a range configured as an array, for example, Excel no longer treats the cells individually. Instead it works with all the cells at once, which enables you to apply a formula to every cell in the range using just a single operation. You create an array either by running a function that returns an array result, or by entering an array formula, which is a single formula that either uses an array as an argument or enters its results in multiple cells.

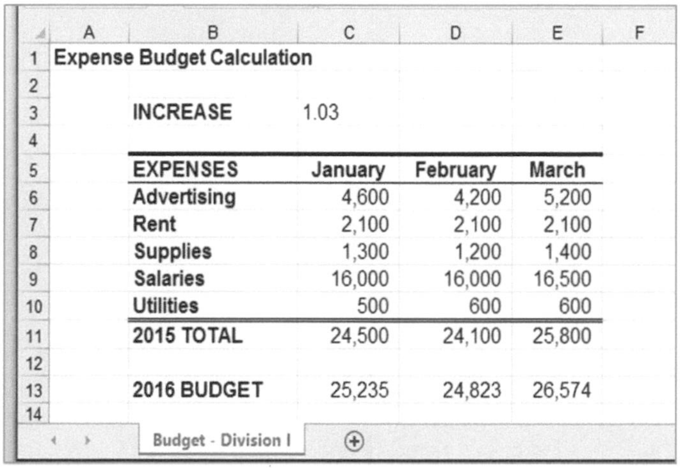

	A	B	C	D	E	F
1	Expense Budget Calculation					
2						
3		INCREASE	1.03			
4						
5		EXPENSES	January	February	March	
6		Advertising	4,600	4,200	5,200	
7		Rent	2,100	2,100	2,100	
8		Supplies	1,300	1,200	1,400	
9		Salaries	16,000	16,000	16,500	
10		Utilities	500	600	600	
11		2015 TOTAL	24,500	24,100	25,800	
12						
13		2016 BUDGET	25,235	24,823	26,574	
14						

Budget - Division I

Figure 13.1: Array Example.xlsx

13.1 Understanding Array Formula

In the worksheet shown in Figure 13.1, the 2016 BUDGET totals are calculated using a separate formula for each month, as shown here:

Total Formula

January 2016 BUDGET =C11*$C$3

February 2016 BUDGET =D11*$C$3

March 2016 BUDGET =E11*$C$3

You can replace the three formulas with a single array formula by following these steps:

1. Select the range you want to use for the array formula. In the 2016 BUDGET example, you would select C13:E13
2. Type the formula and, in the place where you would normally enter a cell reference, type a range reference that includes the cells you want to use. In this example, you would enter **C11:E11*$C$3**
3. Pres **Ctrl+Shift+Enter**

The 2016 BUDGET cells (C13, D13, and E13) now all contain the same formula:

{=C11:E11*$C$3}

In other words, you were able to enter a formula into three different cells using just a single operation.

To understand how Excel processes an array, you need to keep in mind that Excel always sets up a correspondence between the array cells and the cells of the range you enter into the array formula. In the 2016 BUDGET example, the array consists of cells C13, D13 and E13, and the range used in the formula consists of cells C11, D11 and E11. Excel sets up a correspondence between array cell C13 and input cell C11, D13 and D11, and E13 and E11. To calculate the value for cell C13 (the January 2016 BUDGET), for example, Excel grabs the input value from cell C11 and substitute that in the formula as shown in Figure 13.2.

Figure 13.2

Array formula = {C11:E11 * $C$3}		
Array Cell	Input cell from formula	What the formula becomes
C13 →	C11 →	C11 * $C$3
D13 →	D11 →	D11 * $C$3
E13 →	E11 →	E11 * $C$3

<<Fig 13.3>>

Figure 13.3: array exercise single cell.xlsx

Task: We want to use array formula to compute the total sales (Figure 13.3). We could, of course, multiply each unit sold by its corresponding unit price and then sum them to get the grand total. The alternative is to use array formula which acts on the cells as unit. For example, to compute the sales for product AR-998, in cell D2 you would use the formula:

D2: = C2*B2.

To compute the grand total sales (C9), all you need to do is to replace individual cells with ranges. So C2, will be replaced with the range C2:C7 and B2 will be replaced with B2:B7. Remember, in array formulas Excel will treat the range as a unit (as if it were a single cell). So the formula will become C2:C7*B2:B7. But because we are looking for the sum (an aggregate), we have to use an aggregate function, otherwise Excel will be looking for a range. So the grand total formula becomes: SUM(C2:C7*B2:B7)

As an exercise, if you want to use the array formula {C2:C7*B2:B7} (without **SUM**) where will you place the results?

In the previous array formulas, the array arguments have been cell ranges. You also can use constant values as array arguments. The main advantage of using array constants is clean spreadsheet; you don't have to clutter the worksheet with values.

To enter an array constant in a formula, enter the values right in the formula and observe the following guidelines:

- Enclose the values in braces

- If you want Excel to treat the values as a row, separate each value with a comma

- If you want Excel to treat the values as a column, separate each value with a semicolon.

Examples:

The following array constant is equivalent to entering the individual values in a column on the worksheet: {1; 2; 3; 4}

Similarly, the following is equivalent to entering the individual values into a row in your worksheet: {1, 2, 3, 4, 5}

The following produces a 3-column, 2-row data values:

{1, 2, 3; 4, 5, 6}

	A	B	C	D	E	F
1						
2						
3		Principal	$10,000		Payment (Range)	Payment (Array Constant)
4		Term	5		(193)	(193)
5		Rates	6.00%		(194)	(194)
6			6.25%		(196)	(196)
7			6.50%		(197)	(197)
8			6.75%			

Figure 13.4: array constants.xlsx

As a practical example, Figure 13.4 shows two different array formulas. The one on the left (used in range E4:E7) calculates various loan payments, given the different interest rates in the range C5:C8. The array formula on the right (range F4:F7) does the same thing, but the interest rate values are entered as array constants directly into the formula.

13.3 Naming Array Constants

You can create and name an array constant that you can use in formulas. Figure 13.5 shows a named array being created from the New Name dialog box (**Formula Defined Names Define Name**). The name of the array is **DayName**, and refers to the following array constants:

={"Sun","Mon","Tue","Wed","Thu","Fri","Sat"}

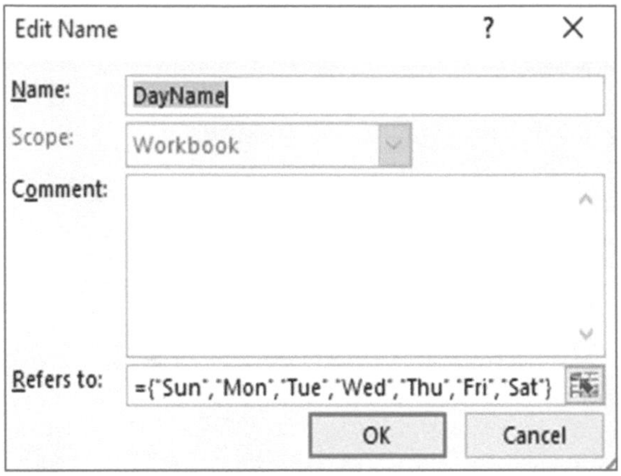

Figure 13.5 Naming Arrays

After creating this named array, you can use it in a formula. Fig 13.6 shows a worksheet that contains a multicell array formula entered into the range B2:H2. The formula is

{=DayName}

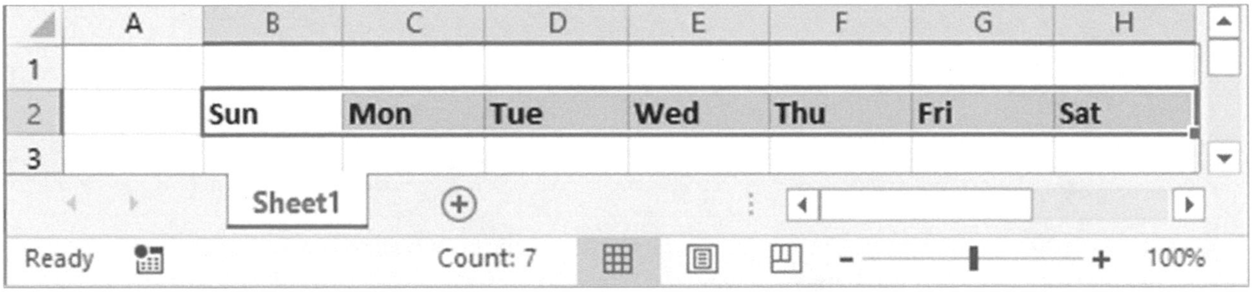

Figure 13.6

You also can access the individual elements from the array by using the Excel INDEX function. The following formula, for example, returns Wed, the fourth item in the DayName array:

=INDEX(DayName, 4)

13.4 Working with Array Formulas

The mechanics of dealing with array formulas, such as entering and editing is slightly different than for ordinary ranges.

13.4.1 Entering an array formula

After entering an array formula into a cell or a range, you must finish with **Ctrl+Shift+Enter**, not just **Enter**.

13.4.2 Selecting an array formula range

You can manually select the cells that contain a multicell array formula by using the normal cell selection procedures. Or you can use either of the following methods:

- Activate any cell in the array formula range, Choose **Home Editing Find & Select Go To** or press F5. The Go To dialog box appears, click the Special button and then choose the Current Array option. Click OK to close the dialog box.

- Activate any cell in the array formula range and press Ctrl+/ (forward slash) to select the cells that make up the array

13.4.3 Editing array formulas

The following rules apply to editing array formulas:

- You can't change the contents of any individual cell that makes up an array formula

- You can't move cells that make up part of an array formula. You can move an entire array

- You can't delete cells. You can delete an entire array

- You can't insert new cells into an array range

- You can't use multicell array formulas inside of a table that was created by choosing Insert ⇒ Tables ⇒ Table. Also you can't convert a range to a table if the range contains multicell array formula.

13.4.4 Expanding or contracting a multicell array formula

Follow these steps if you may need to expand or contract a multicell array:

- Select the entire range of the array formula

- Press F2 to enter Edit mode

- Press Ctrl+Enter. This step enters an identical (non-array) formula into each selected cell

- Change your range selection to include additional or fewer cells, but make sure the active cell is in a cell that is part of the original array

- Press F2 to enter Edit mode

- Press Ctrl+Shift+Enter

13.5 Some Examples of Multicell Array Formulas

The following sections provide examples of additional features of multicell array formulas.

13.5.1 Counting characters in a range

	A	B	C	D
1	aboriginal	10		
2	aborigine	9	Total characters:	112
3	aborting	8		
4	abort	5		
5	abound	6		
6	about	5		
7	above	5		
8	aboveboard	10		
9	aboveground	11		
10	abovementioned	14		
11	abrade	6		
12	abrasion	8		
13	abrasive	8		
14	abreact	7		
15				
16	Total characters	112		

Figure 13.7: counting characters.xlsx

To find the total number of characters in range A1:A14, you can calculate the characters for each cell and them sum them, such as SUM(B1:B14). Or you can use an array formula thus eliminating the intermediate formula:

{=SUM(LEN(A1:A14)}

13.5.2 Using functions with an array

E7			×	✓	f_x	{=SUM(SQRT(A1:C5))}

	A	B	C	D	E	F
1	64	4	100			
2	100	25	9			
3	81	36	1			
4	144	49	4			
5	16	121	25			
6						
7					95	

Figure 13.8

13.5.3 Summing three smallest values in a range

	A	B	C	D	E	F	G	H
1								
2								
3		73	689	55		First smallest	=SMALL(B2:D7,1)	3
4		33	12	90		Second smallest	=SMALL(B2:D7,2)	6
5		55	6	33		Third smallest	=SMALL(B2:D7,3)	12
6		32	94	213				
7		45	3	45		Sum of three smallest	=SUM(H1:H4)	21
8		23	54	64				
9						Using Array Formula:	21	

Figure 13.9: sum three smallest.xlsx

13.5.4 Counting text cells in a range

▲	A	B	C	D	E	F	G
1	sam	5	senior		1	0	1
2	6	paul	90		0	1	0
3	-9	near	43		0	1	0
4	tutu	big man	good		1	1	1
5	2	37	sincere		0	0	1
6	12	78	good		0	0	1
7	sydney	then	come		1	1	1
8	perth	simple			1	1	0
9	67	frank	bring		0	1	1
10							
11						16	

Figure 13.10: counting text cells.xlsx

Also try: SUM(ISTEXT(A1:C9)*1). (Note =TRUE*1 =1)

13.5.5 Eliminating intermediate formulas

▲	A	B	C	D
1	**Student**	**Pre-Test**	**Post-Test**	**Change**
2	Sam	37	83	46
3	Tom	52	83	30
4	Cindy	2	60	58
5	Sally	52	2	-50
6	Gabby	68	37	-30
7	Duo	73	90	17
8	Peter	94	81	-13
9	Nany	19	95	76
10	Grace	23	77	54
11	Mich	84	72	-11
12	Dan	92	60	-32
13	Emma	69	89	20
14	Brown	24	2	-22
15	Josh	18	1	-17
16				
17			Average Change:	76
18			Eliminate intermediate calculation	76

Figure 13.11: Eliminate intermediate formulas.xlsx

13.5.6 More Examples of Array Formulas

This section provides more sophisticated examples of single-cell array formulas

13.5.7 Single-Cell Array Formulas

You enter single-cell array formulas into a single cell (not a range of cells). These array formulas work with arrays contained in a range or that exist in memory.

13.5.8 Summing a range that contains errors

The SUM function doesn't work if you attempt to sum a range that contains an error value (such as #DIV/0 or #N/A).

E13 | {=SUM(IFERROR(D4:D10,""))}

	A	B	C	D	E	F
1	Summing a range that contains error values					
2						
3	ITEM	COST	NUMBER	TOTAL		
4	A-933	10	4	40		
5	A-833	6	4	24		
6	C-902	#N/A	3	#N/A		
7	F-902	#N/A	10	#N/A		
8	J-111	3	12	36		
9	R-234	20	6	120		
10	S-984	5	4	20		
11			TOTAL	#N/A		
12						
13					240	
14						
15				=SUM(D4:D10)		
16	The presence of #N/A in the sum range prodeces the #N/A result					

Figure 13.12: summing a range that contains errors.xlsx

Notice that the array formula first replaces the error cells with blanks before the summation is applied, because the sum function can work with blank cells.

10.3.4.1 Counting the number of error values in a range

	A	B	C	D	E
1	Counting error values in a range				
2					
3	5	5	#DIV/0!	#N/A	
4	6	9	4	#NAME?	
5	9	6	9	9	
6	7	0	0	1	
7	6	5	1	2	
8	9	7	3	9	
9	10	2	10	7	
10	8	7	5	5	
11	3	4	3	5	
12	5	10	3	5	
13	6	8	#NUM!	4	
14	1	0	7	9	
15					
16	Number of error values:				4

Figure 13.13: counting the number of error values in a range.xlsx

In Figure 13.13, the following formula also works:

{=SUM(ISERROR(Data)*1)}

Difference between the **IFERROR** function and **ISERROR** function.

IFERROR

IFERROR substitutes a cell with its second argument if the cell produces an error:

For example, if cell D3 contains an error (say #DIV/0), the following formula in cell D4 will produce "*There is an error!*":

Cell D4: =IFERROR(D3, "There is an error!")

ISERROR

ISERROR Produces TRUE if the cell has an error, otherwise it produces FALSE

For example, if cell D3 has an error (say #DIV/0), the following formula in cell D4 will produce TRUE

Cell D4: =ISERROR(D3)

13.5.6.3 Summing the N largest values in a range

The following array formula returns the sum of the ten largest values in a range named Data:

{=SUM(LARGE(Data, ROW(INDIRECT("1:10"))))}

If the number of cells to sum is contained in cell C17, for example, use the following array:

{=SUM(LARGE(Data, ROW(INDIRECT("1:"&C17))))}

13.5.6.4 Computing an average that excludes zeros

Figure 67 shows a sample worksheet that calculates average sales. The formula in cell B13 is

=AVERAGE(B4:B11)

C14 | *fx* {=AVERAGE(IF(Data<>0,Data))}

	A	B	C	D	E	F
1	Exclude zero from average					
2						
3	Sales Person	Sales				
4	Abner	23,991				
5	Baker	15,092				
6	Charleston	0				
7	Davis	11,893				
8	Ellerman	32,116				
9	Flugelhart	29,089				
10	Gallaway	0				
11	Harrison	33,211				
12						
13	Average with zeros:		18,174			
14	Average without zeros (array formula):		24,232			
15						
16	Uses AVERAGEIF (no array formula):		24,232			
17						
18						

Sheet5

Figure 13.14: computing an average that excludes zeros.xlsx

Two of the sales staff had the week off, however, so including their 0 sales in the average doesn't accurately describe the average sales per representative.

The AVERAGE function ignores blank cells, but it does not ignore cell that contain 0

The following array formula returns the average of the range but excludes the cells containing 0:

{=AVERAGE(IF(B5:B12<>0, B5:B12))}

You can also get the same result with a regular (nonarray) formula:

=SUM(B5:B12)/COUNTIF(B5:B12, "<>0")

> ***NOTE: The only reason to use an array formula to calculate an average that excludes zero values is for compatibility with Excel versions prior to Excel 2007. A simpler approach is to use the AVERAGEIF function in a nonarray formula:***
>
> ***=AVERAGEIF(B5:B12, "<>0", B5:B12)***

13.5.6.5 Determining whether a particular value appears in a range

To determine whether a particular value appears in a single column of cells, you can use the LOOKUP function. But if the range consists of multiple columns, you'll need to use a different approach.

Figure 13.15 shows a worksheet with a list of names in A5:E24 (named ***NameList***). An array formula in cell D3 check the name entered in cell C3 (named ***TheName***). If the name exists in the list of names, the formula displays the text "Found"; otherwise it displays "Not Found"

Figure 13.15: Is a value in a range?

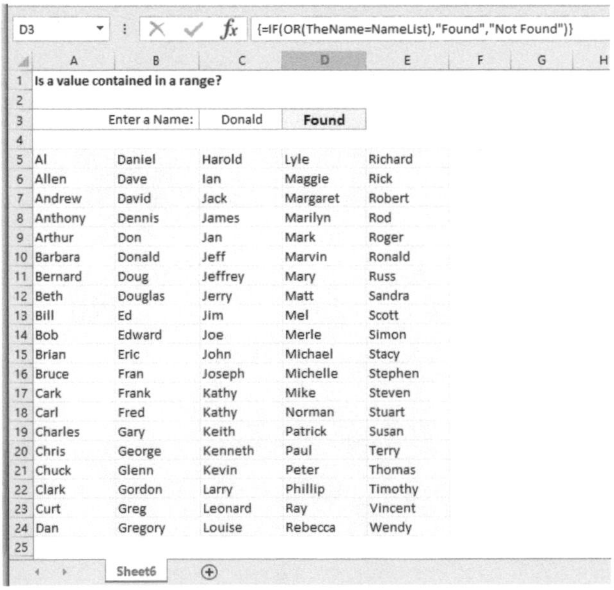

D3 {=IF(OR(TheName=NameList),"Found","Not Found")}

	A	B	C	D	E
1	Is a value contained in a range?				
2					
3		Enter a Name:	Donald	Found	
4					
5	Al	Daniel	Harold	Lyle	Richard
6	Allen	Dave	Ian	Maggie	Rick
7	Andrew	David	Jack	Margaret	Robert
8	Anthony	Dennis	James	Marilyn	Rod
9	Arthur	Don	Jan	Mark	Roger
10	Barbara	Donald	Jeff	Marvin	Ronald
11	Bernard	Doug	Jeffrey	Mary	Russ
12	Beth	Douglas	Jerry	Matt	Sandra
13	Bill	Ed	Jim	Mel	Scott
14	Bob	Edward	Joe	Merle	Simon
15	Brian	Eric	John	Michael	Stacy
16	Bruce	Fran	Joseph	Michelle	Stephen
17	Cark	Frank	Kathy	Mike	Steven
18	Carl	Fred	Kathy	Norman	Stuart
19	Charles	Gary	Keith	Patrick	Susan
20	Chris	George	Kenneth	Paul	Terry
21	Chuck	Glenn	Kevin	Peter	Thomas
22	Clark	Gordon	Larry	Phillip	Timothy
23	Curt	Greg	Leonard	Ray	Vincent
24	Dan	Gregory	Louise	Rebecca	Wendy
25					

Sheet6

The array formula in cell D3 is

{=IF(OR(TheName=NameList),"Found","Not Found")}

The formula compares TheName to each cell in the NameList range. It builds a new array that consists of logical TRUE or FALSE values. The OR function returns TRUE if any of the values in the new array returns TRUE. The IF function uses this result to determine which message to display.

A simpler form of the formula follows. This formula displays TRUE if the name is found. Otherwise, it returns FALSE:

{=OR(TheName=NameList)}

Yet another approach uses the COUNTIF function in a non-array formula:

=IF(COUNTIF(NameList, TheName)>0, "Found", Not Found")

13.5.6.6   Counting the number of differences in two ranges

The following array formula compares two corresponding values in two ranges (named **MyData** and **YourData**) and returns the number of differences in the two ranges. If the contents of the two ranges are identical, the formula returns 0

{=SUM(IF(MyData=YourData, 0,1))}

Figure 13.16 shows an example.

D23			✕ ✓ f_x	{=SUM(1*(MyData<>YourData))}						
	A	B	C	D	E	F	G	H	I	J
1										
2	Counting the number of differences									
3										
4	MyData			YourData						
5	1	34		1	34		FALSE	FALSE	0	0
6	3	35		3	35		FALSE	FALSE	0	0
7	5	36		5	36		FALSE	FALSE	0	0
8	7	37		7	38		FALSE	TRUE	0	1
9	9	38		9	38		FALSE	FALSE	0	0
10	11	39		11	39		FALSE	FALSE	0	0
11	13	40		13	40		FALSE	FALSE	0	0
12	15	41		14	41		TRUE	FALSE	1	0
13	17	42		17	42		FALSE	FALSE	0	0
14	19	43		19	43		FALSE	FALSE	0	0
15	21	44		21	44		FALSE	FALSE	0	0
16	23	45		23	43		FALSE	TRUE	0	1
17	25	46		25	46		FALSE	FALSE	0	0
18	27	47		27	47		FALSE	FALSE	0	0
19	29	48		29	48		FALSE	FALSE	0	0
20	31	49		31	49		FALSE	FALSE	0	0
21	33	50		33	50		FALSE	FALSE	0	0
22	Differences Found:			3						
23	Alternate version:			3						

Figure 13.16: counting the number of differences in two ranges

This formula works by creating a new array of the same size as the ranges being compared. The IF function fills this new array with 0s and 1s: 1 if a difference is found, and 0 if corresponding cells are the same. The SUM function then returns the sum of the values in the array.

The following array formula, which is simpler, is another way of calculating the same result:

{=SUM(1*(MyData<>YourData))}

This version of the formula relies on the fact that TRUE * 1 = 1 and FALSE * 1 = 0

13.5.6.7   Determining whether a range contains valid values

You may have a list of items that you need to check against another list. For example, you may import a list of part numbers into a range named ***myList***, and you want to ensure that all the part numbers are valid. You can do so by comparing the items in the imported list against the items in a master list of part numbers (named Master). Figure 13.17 shows an example. The following array formula returns TRUE if every item in the range named MyList is found in the range called Master. Both ranges must consist of a single column, but they don't need to contain the same number of rows:

{=ISNA(MATCH(TRUE, ISNA(MATCH(MyList, Master,0)),0))}

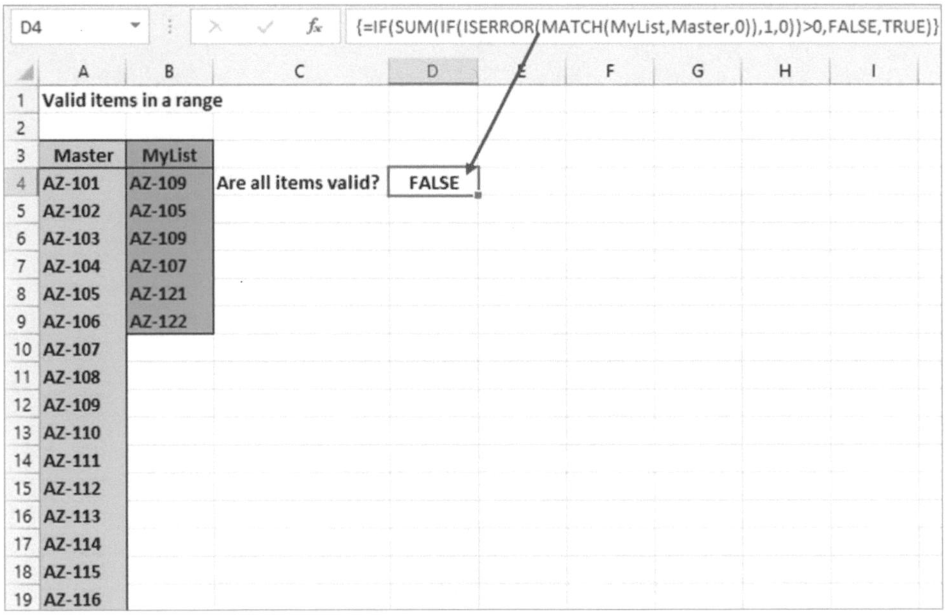

Figure 13.17: Does range contain valid values.xlsx

The array formula that follows returns the number of invalid items. In other words, it returns the number of items in MyList that do not appear in Master:

{=SUM(1*ISNA(MATCH(MyList, Master,0)))}

To return the first invalid item in MyList, use the following array formula:

{=INDEX(MyList, MATCH(TRUE, ISNA(MATCH(MyList, Master, 0)), 0))}

EXERCISE 1

1. Open the *"insert named cells into formulas.xlsx workbook."* In cell C14, write a formula to return the Grand Profit/Loss using the *Income* and *Expenses* named cells. (**First create the named cells "*Income*" in cell B12 and "*Expenses*" in cell C12**)

2. Open the Linked cell.xlsx workbook. Open a second (blank) workbook. In the blank workbook (Sheet1), link cell B1 to cell B12 in the first workbook. Then link cell B2 to cell C12.

3. Close all workbooks. Open a new workbook. Link cell A1 to cell C12 in sheet1 of the Linked cells. xlsx workbook (now closed) *('C:\GrandTotals\Exercises\GT003_Fn\Linked cells.xlsx]!Sheet1!C12)*

EXERCISE 2

1. Open the *"table formula.xlsx."* Convert the data range to a table (choose **My Table Has Headers**). Show the Totals Row. Create a computed column called "*Difference*" as *Actual-Projected*. Show the maximum of the Difference column in the Totals Row.

   a. Turn off the *Automatic creating calculated column* feature
   b. Create another calculated column and observe the effect
   c. Turn on the *Automatic creating calculated column* feature
   d. In an empty cell, write a formula to return the sum of the table (*Table1*)
   e. Remove the **Totals Row**
   f. Convert the table back to range
   g. Calculate the sum of the Actual column
   h. Change the column name to *Actual2015* and observe how the formula adjusts

2. Open the "*Named constants examples.xlsx.*" Create three named constants,

Rate1=0.125; *Rate2*=0.25; *Rate3*=0.5. In cell B2, write the formula:

   a. =IF(A2<500000, A2*Rate1, IF(A2>=1000000, A2*Rate3, A2*Rate2))

Copy the formula down.

If you want to use the logic **AND** operator, you can write the formula in the following way:

=IF(A2<500000,A2*Rate1, IF(AND(A2>=50000, A2<1000000),A2*Rate2, A2*Rate3))

3. Open the "*Named formula.xlsx.*". In cell B12, create a named formula called "*ActualMinusForecast*." (Important: Select Cell B12 before you create the formula). In the Referred To box, write the formula: SUM(C4:C10)-SUM(B4:B10). Copy the formula to C12:F12.

4. Create a table as follows with data:

City	Population	Av. Temperature	Av. Income
Perth			
Sydney			
Adelaide			
Darwin			

Create names with the headers. Use the Excel *Intersection operator* to return the average temperature for Sydney.

5. Open a new workbook. In cell A1, write a formula to return:

Average Expenditure is $7,754.57. Use the **DOLLAR** function and then the **TEXT** function. In cell B4, write a formula to return:

Cell B4: "Date Printed:" Today's Date

Cell B5: "Time of Printing:" Current time

"Date Printed: Today's date. In cell B5

6. Type a serial number and format as Date/Time

7. Open "*Sum Hours Worked.xlsx*". Compute the sum of the hours

You need to format cell B9 to display the correct result

8. Open the "*basic counting.xlsx*" workbook and examine the formulas and results

9. Open the "*hlookupexample.xlsx*". Use the HLOOKUP function to find the tax rate for income of $21,566

10. Open the "*Invoice Template.xlsx*". Fill in *Quantity*: and "*Price*" values. Use array formula to get each extended price and subtotals

11. Open the "*Summing a range that contains errors.xlsx*" workbook. Explain the array formula in cell D13. How will you achieve the same result without using array formula?

Modify the formula in cell D13 to return the sum for the range B4:C10

12. Open a blank workbook. Enter about 15 random values in a rectangular range. Use an array formula to find the sum of the square roots of the range:

{=SUM(SQRT(A1:C5))}

EXERCISE 3

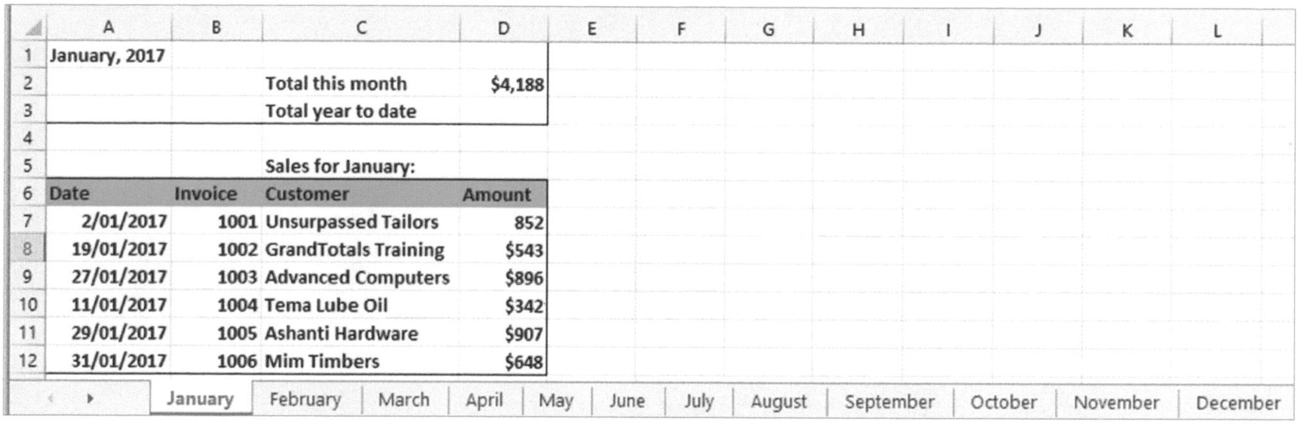

▲	A	B	C	D	E	F	G	H	I	J	K	L
1	January, 2017											
2			Total this month	$4,188								
3			Total year to date									
4												
5			Sales for January:									
6	Date	Invoice	Customer	Amount								
7	2/01/2017	1001	Unsurpassed Tailors	852								
8	19/01/2017	1002	GrandTotals Training	$543								
9	27/01/2017	1003	Advanced Computers	$896								
10	11/01/2017	1004	Tema Lube Oil	$342								
11	29/01/2017	1005	Ashanti Hardware	$907								
12	31/01/2017	1006	Mim Timbers	$648								

January | February | March | April | May | June | July | August | September | October | November | December

Fig 13.18_Ex3

In this exercise, we would like to add a year-to-date total in cell D3 on each worksheet. This is difficult to do without VBA. We will attempt to solve the problem with the INDIRECT function mingled with the TEXT, DATE, and the YEAR functions:

The final formula should look like:

=INDIRECT(TEXT(DATE(YEAR(A1), MONTH(A1)-1,1), "mmmm") & "!D3")+D2

Question: If instead of the full month names (January, February, …. December), we use abbreviated names (Jan, Feb, …. Dec), how should we modify the formula to make it continue to work?

14. Analysing Data with Tables

14.1 Converting a Range to a Table

Excel has many commands that enable you to work with table data. To take advantage of these commands, you must convert your data from a normal range to a table. To convert to a table:

a. Click any cell within the range that you wish to convert to a table. Two choices:
   - To create a table with the default formatting, select **Insert Table** (or Press **Ctrl+T**)
   - To create a table with the formatting you specify, select **Home Format As Table**, then click a table style in the gallery that appears

b. Excel displays the **Create Table** dialog (or **Format as Table** dialog box). The correct range should be selected automatically by Excel. If not, select the range.

c. If the range has column headers, select the **My Table Has Headers** check box

d. d)   Click OK

After a table is converted to a range, Excel makes the following changes to the range as shown in Figure 14.1

- It formats the table cells
- It adds drop-down arrows to each field header
- In the Ribbon, you see a new "***Design***" tab under **Table Tools** whenever you select a cell within the table

	A	B	C	D	E	F	G
1	Current Date:		20-Feb-17				
2	Average number of days overdue for invoive that are late and have amounts of at least $1,000:						21.1
3							
4	Account Name	Account Number	Invoice Number	Invoice Amount	Due Date	Date Paid	Days Overdue
5	Brimson Furniture	10-0009	117321	$2,144.55	19-Jan-17		32
6	Brimson Furniture	10-0009	117327	$1,847.25	01-Jan-17		19
7	Brimson Furniture	10-0009	117339	$1,234.69	19-Feb-17	17-Feb-17	
8	Brimson Furniture	10-0009	117344	$875.50	05-Mar-17	28-Feb-17	
9	Brimson Furniture	10-0009	117353	$898.54	20-Mar-17	15-Mar-17	
10	Chimera Illusions	02-0200	117318	$3,005.14	14-Jan-17	19-Jan-17	
11	Chimera Illusions	02-0200	117334	$303.65	12-Feb-17	16-Feb-17	
12	Chimera Illusions	02-0200	117345	$588.88	06-Mar-17	06-Mar-17	
13	Chimera Illusions	02-0200	117350	$456.21	15-Mar-17	11-Mar-17	
14	Door Stoppers Ltd	01-0045	117319	$78.85	16-Jan-17	16-Jan-17	
15	Door Stoppers Ltd	01-0045	117324	$101.01	26-Jan-17		25
16	Door Stoppers Ltd	01-0045	117328	$58.50	02-Feb-17		18
17	Door Stoppers Ltd	01-0045	117333	$1,685.74	11-Feb-17	09-Feb-17	
18	Emily's Sports Palace	08-2255	117316	$1,584.20	12-Jan-17		39
19	Emily's Sports Palace	08-2256	117337	$4,347.21	18-Feb-17	17-Feb-17	

Figure 14.1

Note: To convert a table back to normal range, select a cell within the table and select Design Convert to Range

The following basic table operations will be demonstrated in class:

- Selecting a record
- Selecting a field
- Selecting the entire table
- Adding a new record anywhere in the table
- Adding a new record at the bottom of the table
- Adding a new field to the right of the table
- Adding a new field anywhere in the table
- Deleting a record
- Deleting a field
- Displaying table totals
- Formatting the table
- Resizing the table
- Renaming a table

14.3 Sorting a Table

Sorting enables data to be viewed in order, for example by customer name, account number, part number, or any other field. You can also sort by multiple fields (e.g. sort by **State**., then by **Customer Name**).

For a quick sort on a single field, there are two choices:

- Click anywhere inside the field, then click **Data**. In the **Sort & Filter** group click the Sort Ascending or the Sort Descending tab
- Pull down the field's drop-down allow

14.3.1 Performing a More Complex Sort

For a more complex sort on multiple fields, follow these steps:

1. Select a cell inside the table
2. Select **Data Sort**. Excel displays the **Sort** dialog box displayed in Figure 14.2

Figure 14.2

3. Use the **Sort By** list to select the field you want to use for the sort
4. Use the **Order** list to select either an ascending or descending sort
5. Optionally, if you want to sort the data on more than one field, click **Add Level**, use the **Then By** list to select the field, and then select a sort order. Repeat for any other field you want to include in the sort (up to 64 sorting levels)

CAUTION:
Be careful when sorting tables that include formulas. If the formula uses relative addresses that refer to cells outside their own records, the new sort order might change the references and produce erroneous results. If your table formulas must refer to cells outside the table, be sure to use absolute addresses.

14.3.2   Sorting a Table in Natural Order

After sorting a table, you may wish to revert the data back to its natural order. After several sort operations, the **Undo** feature may not be able to restore the natural order of the table. The solution is to create a new numeric field (called, for example, **Records**) in which you assign consecutive numbers (1,2,3…) as you enter the data. To restore the table to its natural order, you sort on the Records field.

Note: The Records fields only works if you add it prior to any irrevocable sorting

The following steps add a new field to the table:

1. Select a cell in the field to the right of where you want the new field inserted
2. Select **Home ⇒ Insert ⇒ Table Columns to the Left**
3. Rename the column header

14.3.3   Sorting on Part of a Field

If you wish to sort the data in a field by using part of the field instead of the whole field (e.g. sorting on only the last name in a field that contains both first and last name):

- First you need to create a new column that contains the text you want (e.g. last name):
- Use Excel's text functions: **=RIGHT(D4, LEN(D4) – FIND(" ", D4))** (see Figure 14.3 below)
- You can then sort the table based on the calculated field

	A	B	C	D	E
A4		fx	=RIGHT(D4,LEN(D4)-FIND(" ",D4))		
1					
2					
3	Sorting Field	CustomerID	Company Name	Contact Name	Contact Title
4	Adutwum	ALFKI	Advanced Computers	Peter Adutwum	Sales Rep
5	Nsia	FRANS	GrandTotals Training	Paul Nsia	Sales Associate
6	Tutu	MEMOT	Deloitte Touche	Sam Tutu	Sales Rep
7	Anton	BERGS	Mim Timbers	Mary Anton	Sales Rep
8	Asare	PARIS	Tema Lube Oil	Benneth Asare	Accounting Manager
9	Batusta	TAOME	SGMC	Bernardo Batusta	Marketing Manager
10	Burns	SANTG	Volta River Authority	Helen Burns	Order Administrator
11	Belgium	COMMI	Manu Groupe	Jonas Belgium	Owner
12	Amoah	SFUMSO	Que Delicia	Solom Amoah	Owner
13	Tortor	AKTA	Island Trading	John Tortor	Office Manager

Figure14.3

14.4   Filtering Table Data

You can filter a table to show only a subset of the records in the table.

14.4.1   Using Filter Lists to Filter a Table

When you create a table from a range, Excel automatically turns on the filter feature, which is why you see drop-down arrows in the cells containing the table's column labels. Clicking one of these arrows displays a list of all the unique entries in the column (see Figure 14.4).

	E	F	G	H
1	Contact Title	Address	City	Region
2	Sales Representative	Sort A to Z	Torino	
3	Sales Associate	Sort Z to A	São Paulo	SP
4	Sales Representative	Sort by Color	Berlin	
5	Sales Representative		London	
6	Accounting Manager	Clear Filter From "Address	Rio de Janeiro	RJ
7	Marketing Manager	Filter by Color	Cowes	Isle of Wight
8	Order Administrator	Text Filters	Luleå	
9	Owner	Search	Stavern	
10	Owner	✓ (Select All)	Paris	
11	Sales Manager	✓ 1 rue Alsace-Lorraine	Lander	WY
12	Sales Representative	✓ 12 Orchestra Terrace	London	
13	Accounting Manager	✓ 12, rue des Bouchers	Madrid	
14	Accounting Manager	✓ 120 Hanover Sq.	Charleroi	
15	Marketing Assistant	✓ 184, chaussée de Tournai	São Paulo	SP
16	Marketing Manager	✓ 187 Suffolk Ln.	México D.F.	
17	Marketing Manager	✓ 1900 Oak St.	Strasbourg	
18	Sales Associate	✓ 2, rue du Commerce	Brandenburg	
19	Sales Associate		London	
20	Marketing Assistant	OK Cancel	São Paulo	SP

Figure 14.4

There are two basic techniques you can use in a Filtered list:

1. Deselect an item's check box to hide the item in the table
2. Select the **Select All** item (to deselect all items if they are initially selected), and then select each item you want displayed one at a time

Here are three things to notice about a filtered table:

- A funnel icon is added to the filtered column

- You can see the exact filter by hovering the mouse over the filtered column's drop-down button. Figure 14.5 shows that the table is filtered for the city "**London**" only

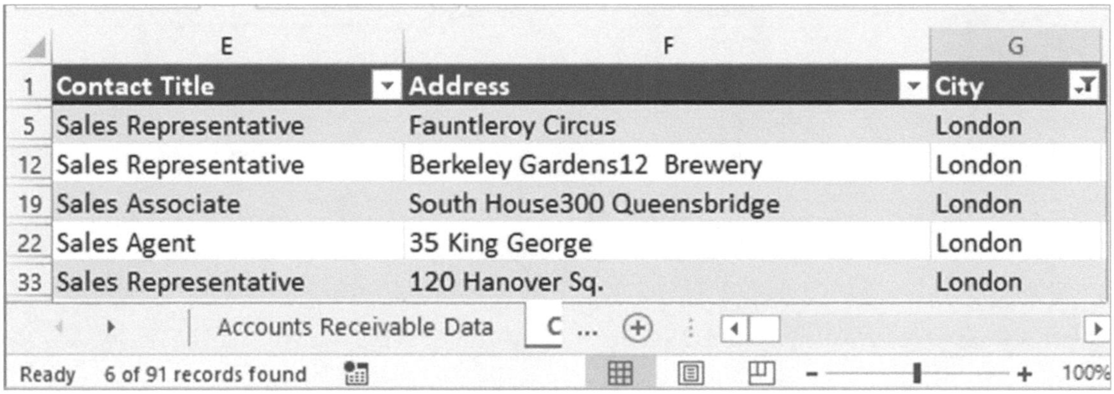

	E	F	G
1	Contact Title	Address	City
5	Sales Representative	Fauntleroy Circus	London
12	Sales Representative	Berkeley Gardens12 Brewery	London
19	Sales Associate	South House300 Queensbridge	London
22	Sales Agent	35 King George	London
33	Sales Representative	120 Hanover Sq.	London

Accounts Receivable Data C …

Ready   6 of 91 records found   100%

Figure 14.5

- You can also see the number of records in the filter at the status bar:

14.4.2   Using Complex Criteria to Filter a Table
Limitations of the Filters features:

Cannot take care of for example, Account Receivable criteria such as:

- Invoices amount greater than $100, less than $1,000, or greater than $10,000

- Account number that begins with 01, 05, or K3

- Days overdue greater than the value in cell G5

To work with these more sophisticated requests, you need to use complex criteria.

14.4.2.1   Setting Up a Criteria Range
A criteria range has some or all of the fields names of the table in the top row, with at least one blank row directly underneath. You enter the criteria in the blank row below the appropriate field headers, and Excel searches the column for records with field values that satisfy the criteria. The following are true about criteria:

- By using either multiple rows or multiple columns, for a single field, you can create compound criteria with as many terms as you like

- Because the criteria are entered into cells, formulas can be used to create computed criteria

- You can place the criteria range anywhere on the worksheet outside the table range. The most common position, however, is a couple of rows above the table range. Figure 14.6 shows a table with a criteria range.

	A	B	C	D	E	F	G
1	Account Name	Account Number	Invoice Number	Invoice Amount	Due Date	Date Paid	Days Overdue
2	Brimson Furniture		>1000				>0
3							
4							
5	Account Name	Account Number	Invoice Number	Invoice Amount	Due Date	Date Paid	Days Overdue
6	Brimson Furniture	10-0009	117321	$2,144.55	19-Jan-13		32
7	Brimson Furniture	10-0009	117327	$1,847.25	1-Feb-13		19
8	Brimson Furniture	10-0009	117339	$1,234.69	19-Feb-13	17-Feb-13	
9	Brimson Furniture	10-0009	117344	$875.50	5-Mar-13	28-Feb-13	
10	Brimson Furniture	10-0009	117353	$898.54	20-Mar-13	15-Mar-13	
11	Chimera Illusions	02-0200	117318	$3,005.14	14-Jan-13	19-Jan-13	
12	Chimera Illusions	02-0200	117334	$303.65	12-Feb-13	16-Feb-13	
13	Chimera Illusions	02-0200	117345	$588.88	6-Mar-13	6-Mar-13	
14	Chimera Illusions	02-0200	117350	$456.21	15-Mar-13	11-Mar-13	
15	Door Stoppers Ltd.	01-0045	117319	$78.85	16-Jan-13	16-Jan-13	
16	Door Stoppers Ltd.	01-0045	117324	$101.01	26-Jan-13		25
17	Door Stoppers Ltd.	01-0045	117328	$58.50	2-Feb-13		18
18	Door Stoppers Ltd.	01-0045	117333	$1,685.74	11-Feb-13	9-Feb-13	

Figure 14.6

14.4.2.2   Filtering a Table with a Criteria Range

To filter a table with a criterion range, follow these steps:

1. Copy the table field names and paste them just above the criteria parameters as shown in Figure 14.6 (It is best to link to the table field name)
2. Below each field name in the criteria range, enter the criteria you want to use
3. Select a cell in the table and then select **Data** ⇒ **Advanced**. Excel displays the **Advanced Filter** dialog box, shown in Figure 14.7
4. Click OK. Excel filters the table as shown in Figure 14.8

Figure 14.7: Advanced Filter

	A	B	C	D	E	F	G
1	Account Name	Account Number	Invoice Number	Invoice Amount	Due Date	Date Paid	Days Overdue
2	Brimson Furniture		>1000				>0
3							
4							
5	Account Name	Account Number	Invoice Number	Invoice Amount	Due Date	Date Paid	Days Overdue
6	Brimson Furniture	10-0009	117321	$2,144.55	19-Jan-13		32
7	Brimson Furniture	10-0009	117327	$1,847.25	1-Feb-13		19

Figure 14.8: Filtered Data

To remove the filter, click the Filter icon in the Sort & Filter group of the Data tab

14.4.3   Entering Computed Criteria

You can create *computed criteria* that use a calculation to match records in the table. The calculations can refer to one or more table fields, or even to cells outside the table, and must return either TRUE or FALSE. Excel selects records that return TRUE

To use compound criteria:

- Add a column to the criteria range and enter the formula in the new field

- Ensure that the name you give to the criteria does not conflict with an existing column name

- When referencing the table cells in the formula, use the first row of the data range

As an example, to select all records in which the **Date Paid** is equal to the **Date Due** in the **Account Receivable** table, create a new column (column H) and enter the following formula:

F8=E8 in cell **H2** and enter "***Paid On Time***" in a new column (H1). ***Note: You don't have to enter a column heading. The criteria are enough.*** Then use the Advanced Filter dialog to filter the data. In this instance, the filter criteria is A1:H2. You can also include other criteria as necessary

The result is shown in Figure 14.9

H2	▼	× ✓	fx	=F6=E6				
	A	B	C	D	E	F	G	H
1	Account Name	Account Number	Invoice Number	Invoice Amount	Due Date	Date Paid	Days Overdue	Pain On Time
2								FALSE
3								
4								
5	Account Name	Account Number	Invoice Number	Invoice Amount	Due Date	Date Paid	Days Overdue	
13	Chimera Illusions	02-0200	117345	$588.88	6-Mar-13	6-Mar-13		
15	Door Stoppers Ltd.	01-0045	117319	$78.85	16-Jan-13	16-Jan-13		

Figure 14.9

> **Note: Use Excel's AND, OR, and NOT functions to create compound criteria. For example, to select all records that meet the following criteria:**

Days Overdue less than 90 **AND** Days Overdue greater than 31

OR

- Account Number is "02-0200"

Use the following formula:

=OR (AND (G6<90, G6>31), B6="02-0200")

14.4.4 Copying Filtered Data to a Different Range

You can filter in Place or ask Excel to place the selected (filtered) data in a range you choose

14.5 Excel's Table Functions

To take your table analysis to a higher level, you can use Excel's table functions, which give you the following advantages:

- You can enter the function into any cell in the worksheet
- You can specify the range the function uses to perform its calculations
- You can enter criteria or reference a criteria range to perform calculations on subset of the table

14.5.1 About Table Functions

The table functions come in two varieties:

- Those that don't require a criteria range
- Those that require a criteria range

14.5.2 Table Functions that Don't Require a Criteria Range

Excel has three table functions that enable you to specify the criteria as arguments rather than ranges: **COUNTIF(), SUMIF(), and AVERAGEIF().**

Using COUNTIF()

The COUNTIF() function counts the number of cells that meet a certain criteria:

Syntax: COUNTIF(*range, criteria*)

Range:	The range of cells to use for the count
Criteria:	The criteria, entered as text, that determines which cells to count.

Excel applies the criteria to *range*

For example, Figure 14.10 shows a COUNTIF () function that calculates the total number of products that have no stock (**Qty On Hand = 0**) in a table named **Inventory**. The formula is:

=COUNTIF (Inventory[Qty On Hand], "=0")

▲	A	B	C	D	E	F	G
2					Products with no stock		29
3							
4	Product Name	Product Code	Qty On Hold	Qty On Hand	Standard Cost	List Price	Value
5	Northwind Traders Chai	NWTB-1	25	25	$13.50	$18.00	$337.50
6	Northwind Traders Syrup	NWTCO-3	0	50	$7.50	$10.00	$375.00
7	Northwind Traders Cajun Season	NWTCO-4	0	0	$16.50	$22.00	$0.00
8	Northwind Traders Olive Oil	NWTO-5	0	15	$16.01	$21.35	$240.19
9	Northwind Traders Boysenberry	NWTJP-6	0	0	$18.75	$25.00	$0.00
10	Northwind Traders Dried Pears	NWTDFN-7	0	0	$22.50	$30.00	$0.00
11	Northwind Traders Curry Sauce	NWTS-8	0	0	$30.00	$40.00	$0.00
12	Northwind Traders Walnuts	NWTDFN-14	0	40	$17.44	$23.25	$697.50
13	Northwind Traders Fruit Cocktail	NWTCFV-17	0	0	$29.25	$39.00	$0.00
14	Northwind Traders Chocolate Bis	NWTBGM-1!	0	0	$6.90	$9.20	$0.00
15	Northwind Traders Marmalade	NWTJP-6	0	0	$60.75	$81.00	$0.00
16	Northwind Traders Scones	NWTBGM-2:	0	0	$7.50	$10.00	$0.00
17	Northwind Traders Beer	NWTB-34	23	23	$10.50	$14.00	$241.50

Figure 14.10

Using SUMIF ()

The SUMIF () function is similar to COUNTIF(), except that it sums the range cells that meet its criteria:

SUMIF (*range, criteria [,sum_range]*)

Range:	*The range of cells to use for the criteria*
Criteria:	*The criteria, entered as text, that determines which cells to sum. Excel applies the criterial to range*
sum_range:	*The range from which the sum values are taken. Excel sums only those cells in sum_range that corresponds to cells in range and meets the criteria. If sum_range is omitted, Excel uses range for the sum*

Figure 14.11 shows a Parts table. The SUMIF() function in cell F16 sums the Total Cost field for the parts where the Division field is equal to 3

F16   *fx*   =SUMIF(Parts[Division], "=3", Parts[Total Cost])

▲	A	B	C	D	E	F	G	H
4								
5	**Parts Database**							
6	Division	Description	Number	Quantity	Cost	Total Cost	Retail	Gross Margin
7	4	Gangley Pliers	D-178	57	$10.47	$ 596.79	$17.95	71.4%
8	3	HCAB Washer	A-201	856	$ 0.12	$ 102.72	$ 0.25	108.3%
9	3	Finley Sprocket	C-098	357	$ 1.57	$ 560.49	$ 2.95	87.9%
10	2	6" Sonotube	B-111	86	$15.24	$1,310.64	$19.95	30.9%
11	4	Langstrom 7" Wrench	D-017	75	$18.69	$1,401.75	$27.95	49.5%
12	3	Thompson Socket	C-321	298	$ 3.11	$ 926.78	$ 5.95	91.3%
13	1	S-Joint	A-182	155	$ 6.85	$1,061.75	$ 9.95	45.3%
14	2	LAMF Valve	B-047	482	$ 4.01	$1,932.82	$ 6.95	73.3%
15								
16				Total cost of Division 3 parts:		$1,589.99		
17				Average gross margin for parts under $10:		81.2%		

Figure 14.11

Using AVERAGEIF()

The AVERAGEIF() function calculates the average of a range of cells that meet its criteria:

AVERAGEIF(range, criteria [, average_range])

range:	The range of cell to use for the criteria
criteria:	The criteria, entered as text, that determines which cells to average. Excel applies the criteria to range
average_range:	The range from which the average values are taken. Excel averages only those cells in *average_range* that correspond to the cells in *range* and meet the criteria. If you omit *average_range*, Excel uses range for the average.

In Figure 11, the AVERAGEIF() function in cell F17 averages the **Gross Margin** field for the parts where the Cost is less than 10. The formula is:

=AVERAGEIF(Parts[Cost], "< 10", Parts[Gross Margin])

15.5.3 Table Functions That Accept Multiple Criteria

Three functions enable multiple conditional aggregate function criteria to be specified:

- **COUNTIFS()**
- **SUMIFS()**
- **AVERAGEIFS()**

These functions are similar to their corresponding single criteria functions.

14.5.4 Table Functions That Require a Criteria Range

Some table functions require a criteria range. These functions have the following syntax:

Dfunction(database, field, criteria)

Dfunction:	The function name, such as **DSUM, DAVERAGE**
Database:	The range of cells that make up the table. You can use either a range name, or the range address
Field:	The name of the field on which you want to perform the operation. You can use either the field name or the field number as the argument (the leftmost Field is 1, the next is 2 etc.). Field names must be in quotation marks (e.g. ("Total Cost")
Criteria:	The range of cells that hold the criteria you want to work with. This can be either a range name or a range address

Using DAVERAGE()

The **DAVERAGE()** function calculates the average field value in the database records that match the criteria. In the Parts database, for example, suppose that you want to calculate the average gross margin for all parts assigned to Division 2:

- Set up a criteria range for the Division field and enter 2 as shown in Figure 14.12
- Enter the following DAVERAGE() function in cell H3

DAVERAGE(Database, "GROSS MARGIN", A2:A3)

| H3 | ▼ : × ✓ ƒx | =DAVERAGE(Database,"Gross Margin",Criteria) |

	A	B	C	D	E	F	G	H
1	**Parts Criteria**							
2	**Division**							
3	2				Average Gross Margin for Division 2:			52.11%
4								
5	**Parts Database**							
6	**Division**	**Description**	**Number**	**Quantity**	**Cost**	**Total Cost**	**Retail**	**Gross Margin**
7	4	Gangley Pliers	D-178	57	$ 10.47	$ 596.79	$ 17.95	71.4%
8	3	HCAB Washer	A-201	856	$ 0.12	$ 102.72	$ 0.25	108.3%
9	3	Finley Sprocket	C-098	357	$ 1.57	$ 560.49	$ 2.95	87.9%
10	2	6" Sonotube	B-111	86	$ 15.24	$ 1,310.64	$ 19.95	30.9%
11	4	Langstrom 7" Wrench	D-017	75	$ 18.69	$ 1,401.75	$ 27.95	49.5%
12	3	Thompson Socket	C-321	298	$ 3.11	$ 926.78	$ 5.95	91.3%
13	1	S-Joint	A-182	155	$ 6.85	$ 1,061.75	$ 9.95	45.3%
14	2	LAMF Valve	B-047	482	$ 4.01	$ 1,932.82	$ 6.95	73.3%

Figure 14.12

Using DGET()

The **DGET()** function extracts the value of a single field in the database records that match the criteria. If there are no matching records, DGET() returns #NUM!

DGET() is typically used to query the table for a specific piece of information. For example, in the Parts table, you might want to know the cost of **Finley Sprocket**. To extract this information, you would first set up a criteria range with the **Description** field and enter **Finley Sprocket**. You would then use the following formula (assuming that the table and criteria range are named ***Parts*** and ***Criteria***):

=DGET(Parts[#All], "Cost", Criteria)

To extract the name of a part that satisfies a certain criterion. For example, to get the part that has the highest gross margin:

1. Set up the criteria to match the highest value in the Gross Margin field
2. Add a DGET() function to extract the description of the matching record

Figure 14.13 shows how this is done. For the criteria, a new field called **Highest Margin** is created. As the text box shows, this field uses the following computed criteria:

=H7=MAX(Parts2[Gross Margin])

	A	B	C	D	E	F	G	H
1	Parts Criteria							
2	Highest Margin	=H7=MAX(Parts2[Gross Margin])						
3	FALSE						Part with Highest Gross Margin:	HCAB Washer
4								
5	Parts Database							
6	Division	Description	Number	Quantity	Cost	Total Cost	Retail	Gross Margin
7	4	Gangley Pliers	D-178	57	$10.47	$ 596.79	$ 17.95	71.4%
8	3	HCAB Washer	A-201	856	$ 0.12	$ 102.72	$ 0.25	108.3%
9	3	Finley Sprocket	C-098	357	$ 1.57	$ 560.49	$ 2.95	87.9%
10	2	6" Sonotube	B-111	86	$15.24	$1,310.64	$ 19.95	30.9%
11	4	Langstrom 7" Wrench	D-017	75	$18.69	$1,401.75	$ 27.95	49.5%
12	3	Thompson Socket	C-321	298	$ 3.11	$ 926.78	$ 5.95	91.3%
13	1	S-Joint	A-182	155	$ 6.85	$1,061.75	$ 9.95	45.3%
14	2	LAMF Valve	B-047	482	$ 4.01	$1,932.82	$ 6.95	73.3%

Figure 14.13

Excel matches only the record that has the highest gross margin. The DGET() function in cell H3 is:

=DGET(Parts2[#All], "Description", A2:A3).

The formula returns the description of the part that has the highest gross margin.

15. Using Excel's Business Modelling Tools

Excel has a plethora of business modelling tools to help with analysing data.

15.1   Using What-If Analysis

What-if-analysis is the most basic method for interrogating worksheet data. With What-If analysis:

- You first calculate a formula, based on the input from variables

- You then change some of the input variables to compute new results

Example:

Figure 15.1 shows a worksheet that calculates the future value of an investment based on five variables: **Interest Rate, Period, Annual Deposit, Initial Deposit, and Deposit Type**. Cell C9 shows the results of the **FV()** function. The following may be considered:

- What if the interest rate is7%?

- What if you deposit $8,000 per year or $12,000?

- What if you reduce the initial deposit?

	A	B	C	D	E	F	G
1							
2		Interest Rate	5%	*The Future Value of an Investment*			
3		Period	10				
4		Annual Deposit	($10,000)				
5		Initial Deposit	($25,000)				
6		Deposit Type	1				
7							
8			Future Value				
9			$172,790				
10							

Figure 15.1

15.1.1   Setting Up a One-Input Data Table

A data table allows you to study the effect of a range of values on a formula. In the figure above, assume you want to see the future value of the investment with the annual deposit varying between $7,000 and $13,000, you could set up a data table as follows:

1. Add to the worksheet the values you want to input into the formula. There are two choices for the placement of these values:
   a. If you want to enter the values in a row, start the row one cell up and one cell to the right of the formula

b. If you want to enter the values in a column, start the column one cell down and one cell to the left of the cell containing the formula, as shown in Figure 15.2

2. Select the range that includes the input values and the formula. (In Figure 15.2, this is **B9:C16**)
3. Select **Data** ⇒ **What-If Analysis** ⇒ **Data Table**. Excel displays the Data Table dialog box
4. How you fill in this dialog box depends on how the data table is set up:
   a. If you entered the input values in a row, use the **Row Input Cell** text box to enter the cell address of the input cell
   b. If the input values are in a column, enter the input cell's address in the **Column Input Cell** text box. In the investment analysis example, you enter **C4 as shown below**

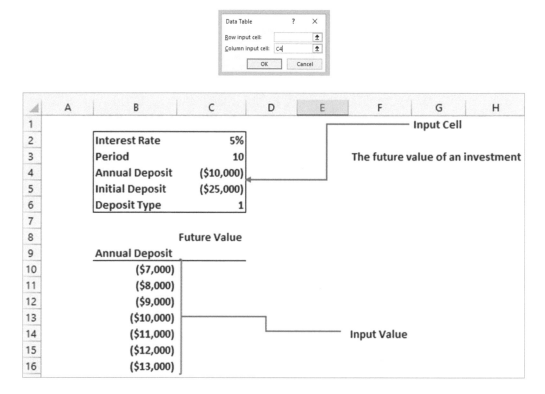

Figure 15.2

Click OK. Excel places each of the input values in the input cell and displays the results in the data table, as shown in Figure 15.3

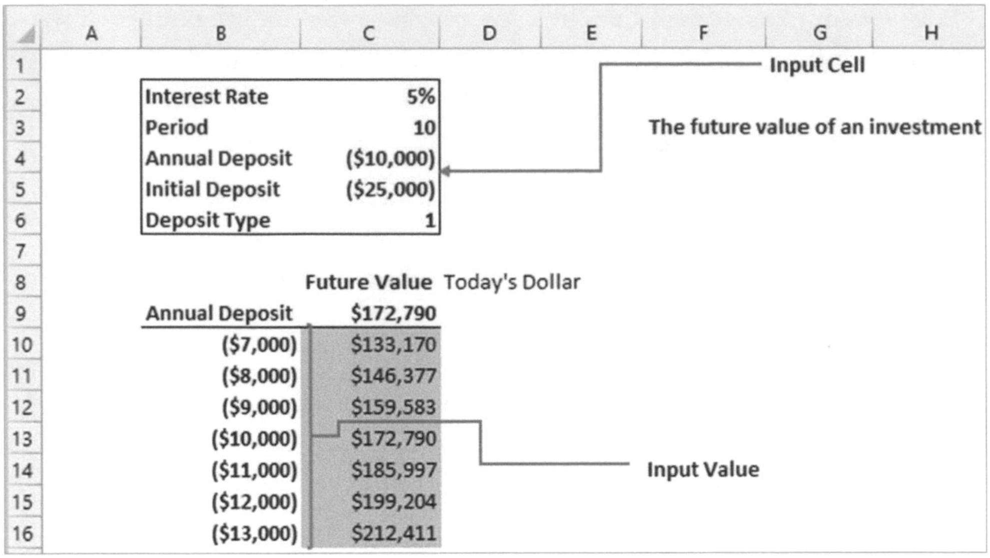

Figure 15.3

15.1.2 Adding More Formulas to the Input Table

You are not restricted to just a single formula in your data table. If you want to see the effect of the various input values on different formulas, you can easily add them to the data table. For example, in the Future Value worksheet, you can factor inflation into the calculation to see how the investment appears in today's dollars. Figure 15.4 shows the revised worksheet with a new inflation variable (cell C7) and a formula that converts the calculated future value into today's dollars (cell D9)

NOTE: This is the formula that converts a future value into today's dollars:

Future Value / (1 + Inflation Rate) ^ Period. Period is the number of years from now that the future value exists

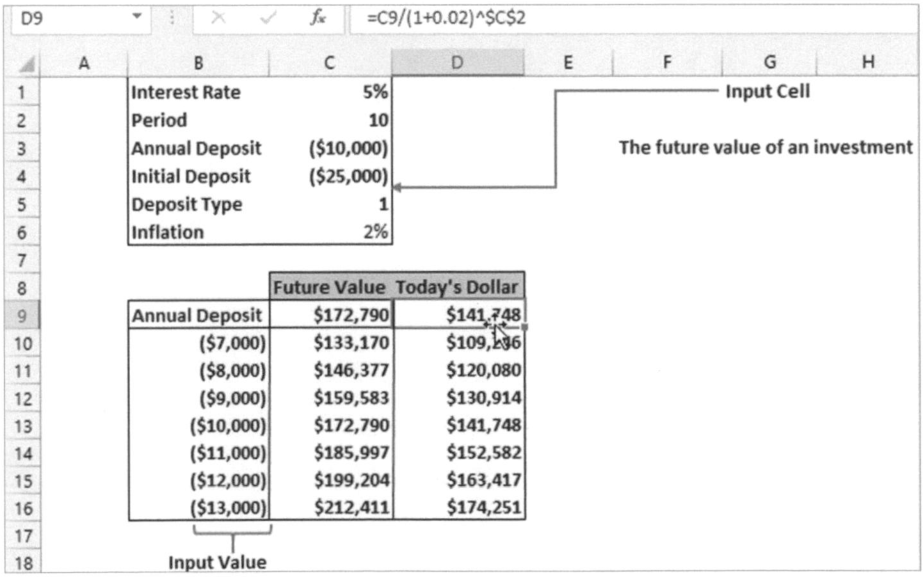

Figure 15.4

120

15.1.3 Setting Up a Two-Input Table

You can also set up a data table that take two input variables. This option enables you to see the effect on the investment's future value when you enter different values – for example, the annual deposit and the interest rate. The following steps show how to set up a two-input data table:

1. Enter one set of values in a column below the formula and the second set of values to the right of the formula in the same row, as shown in Figure 15.5
2. Select the range that includes the input values and the formula (B8:G15 in Figure 15.5)
3. **Select Data ⇨ What-If Analysis ⇨ Data Table.**
4. In the **Row Input Cell** text box, enter the cell address of the input cell that corresponds to the row values you entered (C2 in Figure 15.5 – the interest rate variable)
5. In the **Column Input Cell** text box, enter the cell address of the input cell you want to use for the column values (C4 in Figure 15.5 – the Annual Deposit variable)
6. Click OK. Excel displays the results as shown in Figure 15.6

B8	▼ : ✕ ✓ fx	=FV(C2, C3, C4, C5, C6)				
◢	A	B	C	D	E	F	G

	A	B	C	D	E	F	G
1							
2		Interest Rate	5%	*The Future Value of an Investment*			
3		Period	10				
4		Annual Deposit	($10,000)				
5		Initial Deposit	($25,000)				
6		Deposit Type	1				
7					Interest Rate		
8		$172,790	5%	5.5%	6%	6.5%	7%
9		($7,000)					
10		($8,000)					
11	Annual	($9,000)					
12	Deposit	($10,000)					
13		($11,000)					
14		($12,000)					
15		($13,000)					

Figure 15.5

			Interest Rate			
Interest Rate	5%	*The Future Value of an Investment*				
Period	10					
Annual Deposit	($10,000)					
Initial Deposit	($25,000)					
Deposit Type	1					
			Interest Rate			
$172,790	5%	5.5%	6%	6.5%	7%	
($7,000)	$133,170	$137,788	$142,573	$147,529	$152,664	
($8,000)	$146,377	$151,372	$156,544	$161,901	$167,448	
Annual ($9,000)	$159,583	$164,955	$170,516	$176,272	$182,231	
Deposit ($10,000)	$172,790	$178,539	$184,488	$190,644	$197,015	
($11,000)	$185,997	$192,122	$198,459	$205,016	$211,798	
($12,000)	$199,204	$205,706	$212,431	$219,387	$226,582	
($13,000)	$212,411	$219,289	$226,403	$233,759	$241,366	

Figure 15.6

15.2   Working with Goal Seek

If you know the goal you are seeking (e.g. $50,000) and a single variable to manipulate to get to the goal (e.g. period), you can use **Goal Seek** to reach the goal

15.2.1   How Does Goal Seek Work?

The following pertain to Goal Seek worksheets:

- Formula in one cell

- Formula variable in another cell (with initial value)

- Formula can have many variables, but Goal Seek enables only one variable at a time

- Goal Seek operates by using an *interactive method* to find a solution

15.2.2   Running Goal Seek

To set up Goal Seek:

1. Set up one cell as the changing cell. This is the value that Goal Seek will interactively manipulate to attempt to reach the goal. Enter the initial value into the cell
2. Set up the other input values for the formula and make them proper initial values
3. Create a formula for Goal Seek to use to try to reach the goal

Example:

Goal:	Purchase equipment worth $50,000
Time period for purchase:	5years
Investment Rate:	5% per annum
Problem:	How much annual savings per year to achieve the goal?

Figure 15.7 shows a worksheet set up to use the Goal Seek

- Cell C6 is the changing cell: the annual deposit into the fund (initial value = 0)

- The other cells (C4 and C5) are used as constants for the FV() function
- Cell C8 contains the FV() function that calculates the future value of the equipment fund.

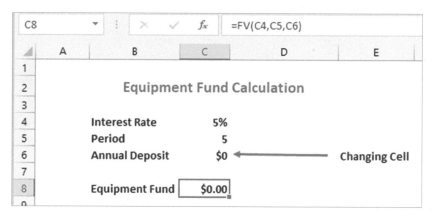

Figure 15.7

To use Goal Seek, follow these steps (refer to Figure 15.7 as you follow these steps):

1. Select **Data** ⇒ **What-If Analysis** ⇒ **Goal Seek**
2. Use the **Set Cell** text box to enter a reference to the cell that contains the formula you want Goal Seek to manipulate (Cell C8)
3. Use the **To Value** text to enter the final value you want for the goal cell (e.g. 50000)
4. Use the **By Changing** Cell text box to enter a reference to the changing cells (cell C6) Figure 15.8 shows a complete Goal Seek dialog box

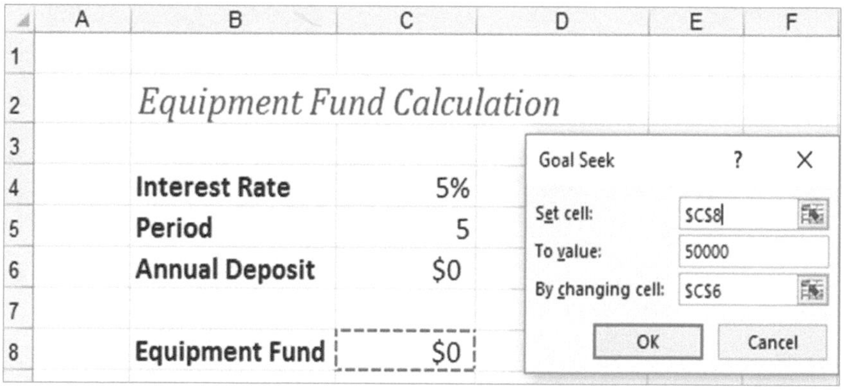

Figure 15.8

5. Click OK. The result of a Goal Seek analysis is shown in Figure 15.9

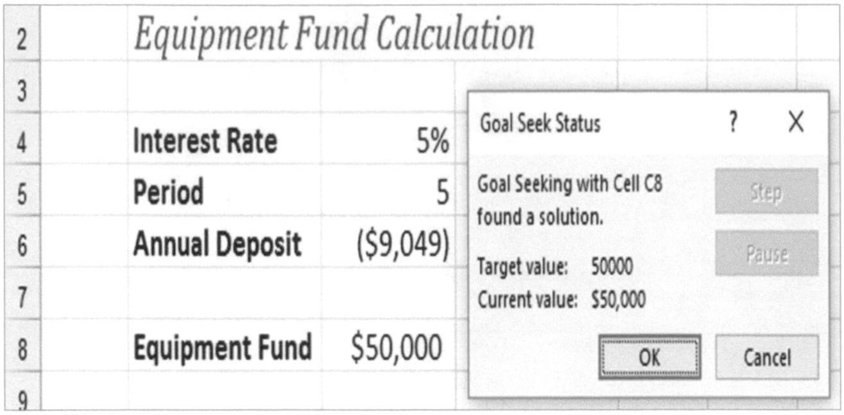

Figure 15.9

15.2.3   Optimizing Product Margin

Problem: **What <u>price</u> will produce 30% margin for the following scenario?**

- Introduction of a new product line

- Product to return a margin of 30% during first year

- Operating conditions:

    - Unit sales during the year to be 100,000

    - Average discount to customers to be 40%

    - Total fixed cost will be $750,000

    - Cost per unit to be $12.63

Figure 24 shows a worksheet set up to handle the situation.

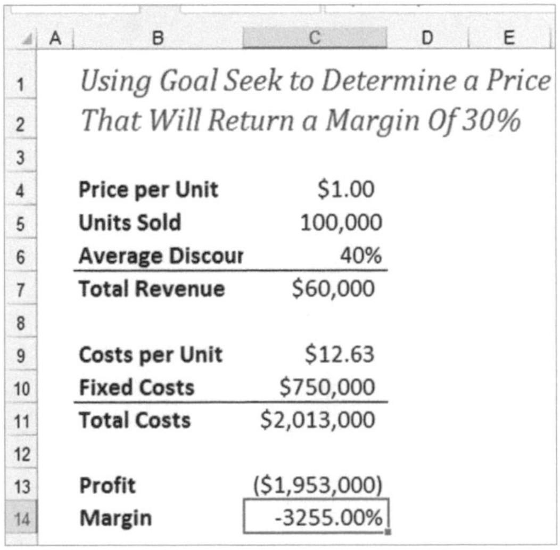

Figure 15.10

- The **Set Cell** reference is C14, the **Margin** calculation

- Enter 0.3 (30%) in the To Value text box

When the Goal Seek is run, it produces a solution of $47.91 for the price, as shown in Figure 15.11

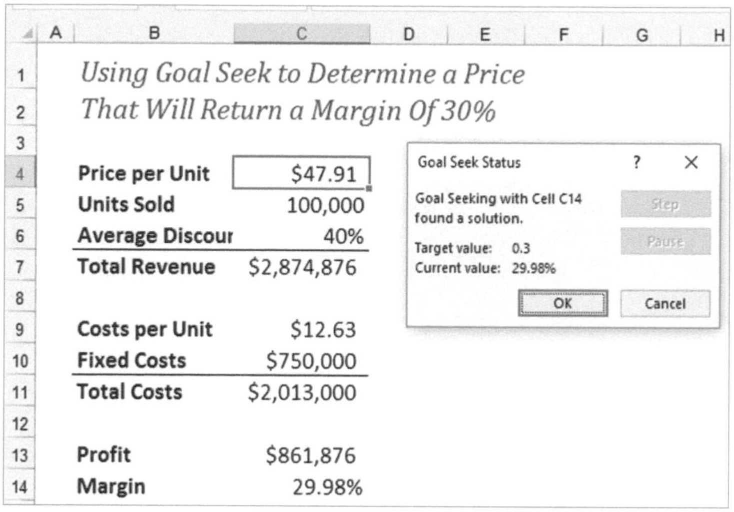

Figure 15.11

15.3 Working with Scenarios

A particular set of guesses (values) and assumptions that you plug into a model is called a scenario. Excels Scenario Manager makes it easy to manage the process of entering different scenarios

15.3.1 Setting Up Your Worksheet for Scenarios

Before creating a scenario:

- Decide which cells in the model will be the input cells. This will be the worksheet variables

- You can have as many as 32 changing cells (variables)

- The changing cells should be constants, not formulas

- Group the changing cells and label them

- For clarity, assign range names to changing cells

15.3.2 Adding a Scenario

To add a scenario to the worksheet, follow these steps:

1. Select **Data** ⇨ **What-If Analysis** ⇨ **Scenario Manager**.
2. Click **Add** on the Scenario Manager dialog box
3. Enter a scenario name in the **Scenario Name** text box
4. Use the **Changing Cell** text box to enter references to the worksheet's changing cells
5. Enter comments if necessary (e.g. description for the scenario)
6. Click OK to display the **Scenario Values** dialog box (see Figure 15.12)

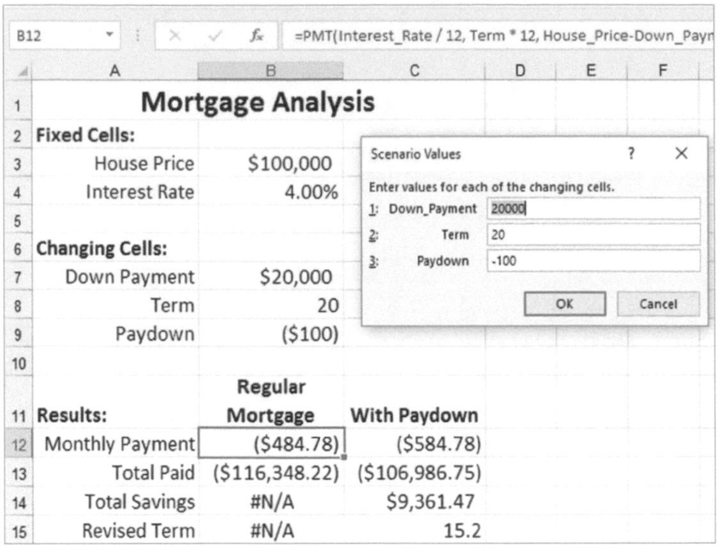

Figure 15.12

Notice in Figure 15.12 that Excel displays the range names for each changing cell (e.g. Terms), which makes it easy to enter your numbers. If the changing cells aren't named, Excel will just display the cell addresses instead.

7. Use the text boxes to enter values for the changing cells
8. To add more scenarios, click **Add** to return to the Add Scenario dialog box and repeat steps 3-7. Or click OK to return to the Scenario Manager dialog box
9. Click Close to return to the worksheet

15.3.3   Displaying a Scenario

After you define a scenario, you can enter its values into the changing cells by displaying the scenario from the Scenario Manager dialog box. The following gives you the details:

1. **Select Data** ⇒ **What-If Analysis** ⇒ **Scenario Manager**
2. In the list of scenarios, select the scenario you wish to display
3. Click **Show**. Excel enters the scenario values into the changing cells. See Figure 15.13

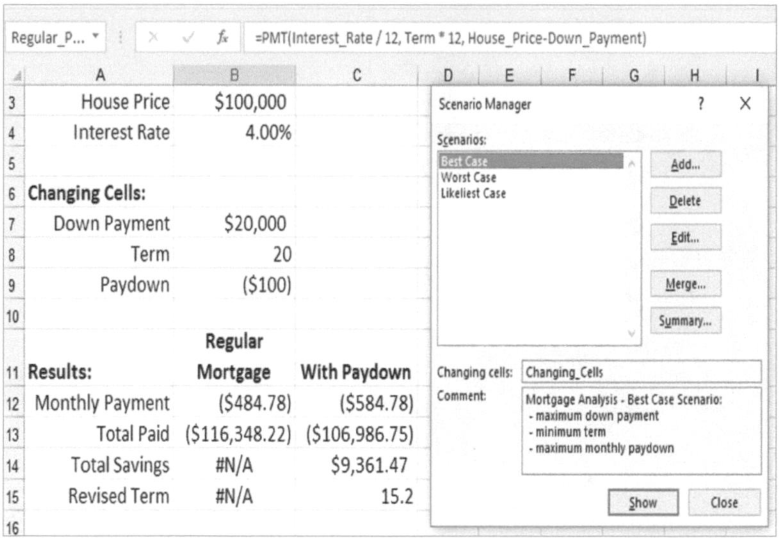

Figure 15.13

15.3.4   Editing a Scenario

If you need to make changes to the scenario (change name, change variable cells etc.), follow these steps:

1. **Select Data** ⇒ **What-If Analysis** ⇒ **Scenario Manager**
2. In the Scenarios list, select the scenario you wish to edit
3. Click Edit
4. Make the required changes and click OK
5. Click Close

15.3.5   Generating a Summary Report

You can create a summary report that shows the changing cells in each of your scenarios along with selected result cells. This allows different scenario results to be compared. To do this follow these steps:

1. **Select Data** ⇒ **What-If Analysis** ⇒ **Scenario Manager**
2. Click **Summary.** Excel displays the **Scenario Summary** dialog box
3. In the **Report Type** group, click either **Scenario Summary** or **Scenario PivotTable Report**
4. In the **Results Cell** box, enter reference to the result cells that you want appear in the report (see Figure 15.14), separating non-contiguous cells with commas

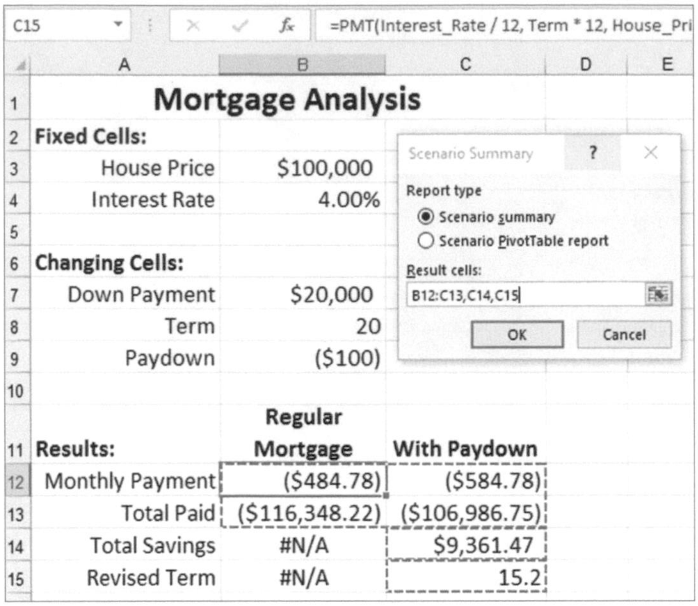

Figure 15.14

5. Click OK

Figure 15.15 shows a sample scenario summary. The names shown in column C (**Down Payment**, **Terms** etc.) are the range names assigned to each changing cell and result cell

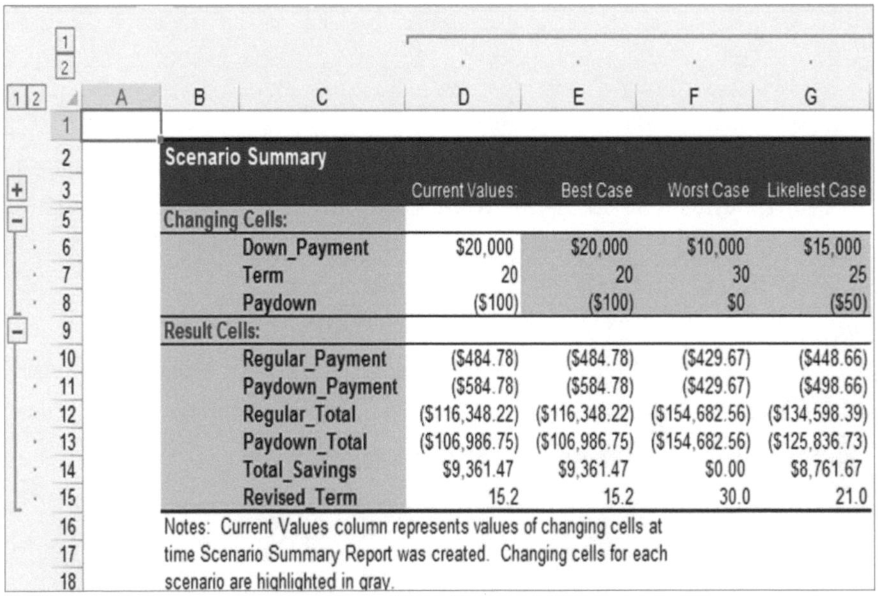

Scenario Summary	Current Values:	Best Case	Worst Case	Likeliest Case
Changing Cells:				
Down_Payment	$20,000	$20,000	$10,000	$15,000
Term	20	20	30	25
Paydown	($100)	($100)	$0	($50)
Result Cells:				
Regular_Payment	($484.78)	($484.78)	($429.67)	($448.66)
Paydown_Payment	($584.78)	($584.78)	($429.67)	($498.66)
Regular_Total	($116,348.22)	($116,348.22)	($154,682.56)	($134,598.39)
Paydown_Total	($106,986.75)	($106,986.75)	($154,682.56)	($125,836.73)
Total_Savings	$9,361.47	$9,361.47	$0.00	$8,761.67
Revised_Term	15.2	15.2	30.0	21.0

Notes: Current Values column represents values of changing cells at time Scenario Summary Report was created. Changing cells for each scenario are highlighted in gray.

Figure 15.15

Figure 15.16 shows the Scenario PivotTable report for the Mortgage Analysis worksheet

Row Label	Regular_Payment	Paydown_Payment	Regular_Total	Paydown_Total	Total_Savings	Revised_Term
1	Changing Cells by		(All)			
2						
3	Row Label	Regular_Payment	Paydown_Payment	Regular_Total	Paydown_Total	Total_Savings	Revised_Term
4 Best Case	-484.7842634	-44358.85165	-50432.2686	-28805.29599	55211.02721	55740.04
5 Likeliest Case	-448.6613143	-44786.1706	-70206.80138	-13369.27027	52452.63317	43622.6347
6 Worst Case	-429.6737659	-76752.55809	-95147.03881	-46546.46665	94581.77804	30

Figure 15.16

The PivotTable's page field – labelled **Changing Cells By** – enables you to switch between scenarios created by different users. If no other users have access to this workbook, you will see only your name in this list.

15.3.6   Deleting a Scenario

You may delete scenarios by:

1. **Select Data** ⇨ **What-If Analysis** ⇨ **Scenario Manager**
2. Select the scenario to be deleted
3. Click Delete and click Close

EXCEL EXERCISES

EXERCISE 1: QUESTIONS

Ex1_Q1.

Encrypt the workbook so that it requires a password to open. Use **GrandTotals** as the password. Mark the workbook as final.

Notes:

_____

_____

_____

_____

_____

Ex1_Q2.

Share the current workbook so that change history is saved for **90 days**. Update the changes automatically every **10 minutes**

Notes:

_____

_____

_____

_____

_____

Ex1_Q3.

Display all the changes that have ever been made by **<u>anyone</u>** to this document and **not** by **when**, **who** or **where**. Don't Highlight the changes on the screen and List the changes on a new sheet

Notes:

_____

_____

_____

_____

_____

_____

Ex1_Q4.

Configure Excel to enable background checking and display detected formula errors in Red.

Notes:

_____

_____

_____

_____

_____

_____

Ex1_Q5.

In the **Family Budget** worksheet, add watches to the **Total row** in Difference column in each set of the **Housing**, **Transportation**, **Loans** and **Entertainment** data

Notes:

_____

_____

_____

_____

_____

_____

Ex1_Q6.

Show all formulas in the **Family Budget** worksheet

Notes:

_____

_____

_____

_____

_____

_____

Ex1_Q7.

In the **Employment Status** worksheet, enable the iterative calculation formula option and set the maximum iterations to be **25** and change to **0.005**

Notes:

_____

_____

_____

_____

_____

Ex1_Q8.

In the **Employee Records** worksheet, use a **COUNTIFS** statement in cell **F6** to count how many employees are in the **Perth Office**.

Notes:

_____

_____

_____

_____

_____

Ex1_Q9.

In the **Sale Orders** worksheet, use an **AVERAGEIFS** statement in **G7** to find the average unit price of **ItemSKUs** greater than **30000**. Do not include Quantities of 0.

Notes:

_____

_____

_____

_____

_____

Ex1_Q10.

In the **Sale Orders** worksheet, create a **SUMIFS** function in **F7** that will return the Quantity total of the **ItemSKU** numbers in the **10000** range.

Notes:

_____

_____

_____

_____

_____

Ex1_Q11.

In the **Employee Records** worksheet, in cell F7 add a function that counts how many people work in the **Darwin** Office.

Notes:

_____

_____

_____

_____

_____

_____

Ex1_Q12.

Create a new worksheet named **Office Expenses**, place the sheet right after **Office Records**. In the new worksheet, in cell **A1** enter the column title **Expenses**. In cell **A2** consolidate the data in the **Office Records** worksheet from cells **A10:B23**, **E10:F23**, **A30:B43**, **E30:F43**, **A50:B63**, **E50:F63** and **A70:B83** using the **SUM** function. Add the labels from the left column.

Notes:

_____

_____

_____

_____

_____

Ex1_Q13.

In the **Employment Status** worksheet, use the **Evaluate Formula** tool to find and correct the error in **S12**.

Notes:

_____

_____

_____

_____

_____

Ex1_Q14.

In the **Employee Records** worksheet, in cell F7 create a **VLOOKUP** function that finds the **ID** for Supervisor **Sam Tutu**.

Notes:

_____

_____

_____

_____

_____

Ex1_Q15.

In the **Status Chart** worksheet, change the **chart layout** to **Layout 1**, change the **chart title** to **Employment History** and change the **chart style** to **Style 9.** Save the chart as a chart template to the **PureSoftwareTemplate** folder in your documents folder and with the name **EmploymentChart**

Notes:

_____

_____

_____

_____

_____

_____

Ex1_Q16.

In the **Financial Services** worksheet, add a Logarithmic Trendline based on 2005 to the **Financial Data** chart that forecasts **1.5** periods into the future. Add an Exponential Trendline to the **Other Data** chart based on 2005.

Notes:

_____

_____

_____

_____

_____

Ex1_Q17.

In the **Office Records** worksheet, modify the data validation input message for the title **Office Records** to be **Our office's income and expenses**.

Notes:

_____

_____

_____

_____

_____

Ex1_Q18.

In the **Family Budget** worksheet, create and show two scenarios named **Wants** and the other named **Wishes**, that allows you to change the **Wanting to Make** value to be **10,000** and **15,000** and show **Wants** in the cell.

Notes:

_____

_____

_____

_____

_____

Ex1_Q19.

Create a new worksheet named **Cut Costs**. In cell A1 of the new worksheet, consolidate the data from the **Family Budget** worksheet using the data in cells **A6:D17**, **A21:D29**, **A33:D39** and **A43:D49**. Set the labels to be used from the **Top Row** and **Left Column**.

Notes:

_____

_____

_____

_____

_____

_____

Ex1_Q20.

Create a PivotTable in a new worksheet from the data in the **Employee Records** sheet. Display the **Office** column as the Report Filter, and **Status** as a Column Label. In the **Row Labels** field, insert the following in the same order: **ID** and **First & Last Name.** Rename the new Sheet **PivotTable**

Notes:

_____

_____

_____

_____

_____

_____

Ex1_Q21.

Create a PivotChart on a <u>new worksheet</u> that displays the data from the **Employee Records** sheet. Do not show the **First & Last Name** field in the report. Make **Status** a Legend Field, **Office** an Axis Field, and **Sum of ID** a Value field.

Notes:

_____

_____

_____

_____

_____

Ex1_Q22.

In the **Employee Records Table** worksheet, rearrange the PivotTable Fields to not show **Office** in any field and show in order: **Status**, **First & Last Name** and **ID** in the **Row Labels** field.

Notes:

_____

_____

_____

_____

_____

Ex1_Q23.

In the **Employee Records Table** worksheet, insert a **slicer** for the **Office** field. Change the **Slicer Caption** to read **Offices Shown**. Use the slicer to filter the PivotTable to only show records from Offices in **Sydney**, **Perth**, and **Melbourne**.

Notes:

_____

_____

_____

_____

_____

Ex1_Q24.

In the **Financial Services** worksheet, create a macro that formats the Row Height to be **30** points and changes the font size to **12**. Name the macro **Height**, and store it in this workbook. Run this macro in the cell range **A3:G9**

Notes:

_____

_____

_____

_____

_____

Ex1_Q25.

In the **Financial Services** worksheet, create a macro that applies a <u>Currency number format</u> and a <u>Blue Gradient Data Bar</u> rule. Name the macro **Formatting**, and store it in only this workbook. Apply the macro to the data in the **Financial Data** (Note: Accept all other default settings.)

Notes:

_____

_____

_____

_____

_____

Ex1_Q26.

In the **Family Budget** worksheet, in any open cells create a <u>Button Form Control</u> named **Set Data Bars**, and assign the button to the **Set_Data_Bars** macro and run it.

Notes:

_____

_____

_____

_____

_____

Ex1_Q27.

In the **Sales Orders** worksheet, modify the <u>Spin Button</u> values to be between **1** and **100** and change in increments of **1**.

Notes:

_____

_____

_____

_____

_____

Ex1_Q28.

In the **Sale Orders** worksheet, map the XML table elements with the name being **NewOrders**, to also **Overwrite** the existing data with new data and **Adjust column width**. Then <u>export</u> the current worksheet as XML data file named **NewOrdersXML** in the **PureSoftwareTemplate** folder in your Documents folder.

Notes:

_____

_____

_____

_____

_____

Ex1_Q29.

Create a custom document property named **Completed** with the Type **Yes or No** with the value set as **No**

Notes:

_____

_____

_____

_____

_____

_____

EXERCISES 1 ANSWERS

Ex1_Q1.

1. Click the **File** tab

2. In **Info**, select **Protect Workbook**. Choose **Encrypt with Password**.

3. Type in **PureTraining** as the password and click **Ok**. Type **PureTraining** again to verify the password, and click **OK**.

4. Select the drop down for **Protect Workbook** and click **Mark as Final**

5. Click **Ok**

Ex1_Q2

1. In the **Review** tab, locate the **Changes** group, and select **Share Workbook**.

2. In the **Advanced** tab, locate **Track Changes**. Keep the history for **90** days.

3. Under **Update Changes**, choose **Automatically every:** and choose **10** minutes

4. Click **Ok**

Ex1_Q3.

1. In the **Review** tab, locate the **Changes** group and select the **Track Changes** drop down. Select **Highlight Changes...**

2. In the **Highlight Changes** dialogue box, make sure **When: Who:**, and **Where:** are unchecked. Uncheck **Highlight changes on screen**.

3. Check **List changes on a new sheet**

4. Click **OK**

Ex1_Q4.

1. In the **File** tab, click **Options**. Select the **Formulas** tab.

2. Under **Error Checking**, click to **Enable background error checking**.

3. Change the colour drop down to **Red**

4. Click **Ok**

Ex1_Q5

1. In the **Formulas** tab, **Formula Auditing** group, select **Watch Window**

2. Click **Add watch...**

3. Select cell **D:18** and click **Add**

4. Repeat steps 2 and 3, using cells **D30**, **D40**, and **D50**

Ex1_Q6

1. In the **Formulas** tab, locate the **Formula Auditing** group and select **Show Formulas**

Ex1_Q7

1. In the **File** tab, select **Options**, and choose the **Formulas** tab

2. Under **Calculation Options**, check **Enable iterative calculations**

3. In **Maximum iterations**, enter **25**, and in **Maximum change** enter **.005**

4. Click **Ok**

Ex1_Q8

1. In the **Employee Record** worksheet, select cell **F6**. Select the **Formulas** tab, locate the **Function Library** group, and select **Insert Function**.

2. Search for **COUNTIFS**, and select it.

3. In **Criteria range 1:** select or type **B7:B39**. In **Criteria:** type **employee**.

4. In **Criteria range 2:** select or type **D7:D39**. In **Criteria** type **Perth**.

5. Click **Ok**.

Ex1_Q9

In the Sale Orders worksheet, use an AVERAGEIFS statement in G7 to find the average unit price of ItemSKUs greater than 30000. Do not include Quantities of 0.

1. In the Formulas tab, locate the Function Library group, and click Insert Function.

2. In the Search box, type AVERAGEIFS, select it from the results, and click OK

3. In the Average range box, enter D5:D24.

4. In the Criteria_range1 box, enter B5:B24

5. In the Criteria1 box, enter ">30000"

6. In the Criteria_range2 box, enter C5:C24

7. In the Criteria2 box, enter ">0"

8. Click OK

Ex1_Q10.

1. In the **Sale Orders** worksheet, select cell **F7**. In the **Formulas** tab, go to the **Function Library** group and click **Insert Function**.

2. In the **Insert Function** window, enter **SUMIFS** and click **Go**. Select **SUMIFS** from the **Select a function** section and click **OK**.

3. In the **Sum_range** field select or enter **C5:C24**

4. In the **Criteria_range1** field select or enter **B5:B24**

5. In the **Criteria1** field enter **>10000**

6. In the **Criteria_range2** field select or enter **B5:B24**

7. In the **Criteria2** field enter **<20000**

8. Click **OK**.

Ex1_Q11.

1. Click **Employee Records** Worksheet and select cell **F7**

2. In the **Formulas** tab, locate the **Function Library** group, and select **Insert Function**. Search for and select **Countif**.

3. In **Range**, type or select **D7:D39**, and in **Criteria** type **Darwin**. Click **Ok**

Ex1_Q12.

1. Click the **Insert Worksheet** button. In the new worksheet, right click on **Sheet2** and click **Rename**. Type in **Office Expenses**. Click and drag the sheet to be right behind Office Records.

2. In the **Office Expenses** worksheet, in cell **A1** and enter <u>**Expenses**</u>. Click into cell **A2** In the **Data** tab, locate the **Data Tools** group, and select **Consolidate**.

3. In the **Consolidate** dialogue box, make sure that **SUM** is in the **Function** drop down. Click in the **Reference** area.

4. Select the **Office Records** worksheet. On the worksheet, select cells **A10:B23**. Click **Add**

5. Repeat step 4 for **E10:F23**, **A30:B43**, **E30:F43**, **A50:B63**, **E50:F63** and **A70:B83**

6. Under **Use Labels in**, check **Left Column**. Click **Ok**

Ex1_Q13

1. Select Cell **S12**. In the **Formulas** tab, locate the **Formula Auditing** group, and click **Evaluate Formula**.

2. The formula in the cell is located in the **Evaluation:** box. Click the **Evaluate** button. The underlined portion of the formula is evaluated each time that the evaluate button is clicked.

3. Click the **Evaluate** button twice. Notice that the Formula is subtracting **67895** from **50509**. The Total row should be adding, not subtracting. This is the error in the formula.

4. Click **Close** in the **Evaluate Formula** window.

5. Edit the Formula in cell **S12** to add the 3 cells instead of subtract.

Ex1_Q14.

1. In the **Employee Records** worksheet, select cell **F7**. In the **Formulas** tab, go to the **Function Library** group and click **Insert Function**.

2. In the **Insert Function** window, enter **VLOOKUP** and click **Go**. Select **VLOOKUP** from the **Select a function** section and click **OK**.

3. In the **Lookup_value** field enter <u>**Sam Tutu**</u>

4. In the **Table_array** field select or enter **A7:D39**

5. In the **Col_index_num** field enter **3**

6. Click **OK**.

Ex1_Q15.

1. Select the **Status Chart** worksheet. On this worksheet, select the chart

2. Click **Chart Tools Design Chart Layouts** group and click the **Quick Layout** dropdown, and select **Layout 1**

3. Click on **Chart Title** and type "**Employment History**"

4. In the **Chart Tools Design** tab, locate the **Chart Styles** group and click the drop down. Select **Style 9**

5. Right click the chart and click **Save as Template**. Navigate to the **PureSoftwareTemplate** folder in your documents folder, name the template **EmploymentChart** and click **Save**.

Ex1_Q16.

1. Click on the **Financial Data** chart, then click on the **Chart Elements** Flyout. Click the Flyout for **Trendline**, and click **More Options**.

2. Select the **2005** series, and click **OK**

3. In the **Format Trendline options**, select **Logarithmic** for the type. Under **Forecast**, type in **1.5** for **Forward**.

4. Select the **Other Data** chart, then click on the **Chart Elements** Flyout. Click the Flyout for **Trendline**, and click **Exponential**.

5. Select the **2005** series, and click **OK**

Ex1_Q17.

1. In the **Office Records** worksheet, select the title **Office Records**, which is cells **A4:G4**.

2. In the **Data** tab, **Data Tools** group, select the drop-down menu for **Data Validation**, and click on **Data Validation...**

3. Select the **Input Message** tab. Under **Input message:** type **Our office's income and expenses**. Leave all other values as they are.

4. Click **OK**

Ex1_Q18.

1. In the **Family Budget** worksheet, in the **Data** tab, go to the **Data Tools** group, click the **What-If Analysis** drop down and select **Scenario Manager**.

2. In the **Scenario Manager** window, click **Add**.

3. In the **Add Scenario** window, in the **Scenario name** enter <u>Wants</u> and in the changing cell select or enter **G22** and click **OK**.

4. In the **Scenario Values** window, enter <u>10000</u> and click **OK**.

5. Repeat steps 2 to 4, using the **scenario name <u>Wishes</u>** and the value <u>15000</u>

6. In the **Scenario Manager**, under the **Scenarios** section, highlight <u>Wants</u>, click **Show** and click **Close**.

Ex1_Q19.

1. Click the **New Sheet** button. In the new worksheet, right click on **Sheet2** and click **Rename**. Type in <u>Cut Costs</u>.

2. In the <u>Cut Costs</u> worksheet, click cell **A1**. In the **Data** tab, locate the **Data Tools** group, and select **Consolidate**.

3. In the **Consolidate** dialogue box, make sure that **Sum** is in the **Function** drop down. Click in the **Reference** area.

4. Select the **Family Budget** worksheet. On this worksheet, select cells **A6:D17**. Click **Add**

5. Repeat step 4 for **A21:D29**, **A33:D39**, and **A43:D49**

6. Under **Use Labels** in, check **Top Row** and **Left Column**. Click **Ok**

Ex1_Q20.

1. In the **Employee Records** worksheet, in the **Insert** tab, go to the **Tables** group, click the **PivotTable** drop down and select **PivotTable**.

2. In the **Select a table or range** field select **A6:D39**. In the **Choose where you...** section select **New Worksheet** and click **OK**.

3. In the new worksheet, in the **PivotTable Field List**, click and drag **Office** to the **Filter** group down below. Click and drag **Status** to the **Column** group, and drag **ID** and **First & Last Name** to the **Row** group.

4. Right click on the new worksheet, click **Rename** and enter <u>PivotTable</u>.

Ex1_Q21.

1. Select the Data in the **Employee Records** sheet, Cell range **A6:D39**. In the **Insert** tab, locate the **Charts** group, click the **PivotChart** dropdown, and select **PivotChart**. In the Create PivotChart window, click **OK**

2. In the **PivotChart Fields** box, Drag and Drop the **Status** field into the **Legend Fields (Series)** box.

3. Drag and Drop the **Office** field into the **Axis Fields (Categories)** box.

4. Drag and Drop the **ID** field into the **Values** box. This field will automatically change to **Sum of ID**.

5. Be sure the **First and Last Name** field is unchecked.

Ex1_Q22.

1. In the **Employee Records Table**, select anywhere in the PivotTable.

2. In the **Pivot Table Field List**, uncheck **Office**.

3. Drag **Status** from **Column Label** to **Row Label**, **First and Last Name** from **Reports Filter** to **Row Label**, and **Sum of ID** from **Values** to **Row Labels** (this will automatically convert to **ID**).

Ex1_Q23.

1. Select any part of the PivotTable. In the **PivotTable Tools/Analyze** tab, locate the **Filter** group, and click **Insert Slicer.**

2. In the **Insert Slicers** window, check the box for **Office**, and click **OK**

3. In the **Slicer Tools/Options** tab, locate the **Slicer** group, and enter **Offices Shown** in the **Slicer Caption** box.

4. In the **Slicer** window, select only **Arizona**, **Utah**, and **Washington**

Ex1_Q24.

1. In the **View** tab, locate the **Macros** group, click the **Macros** dropdown, and select **Record Macro.**

2. In the **Macro name:** box, enter **Height**. Leave the Shortcut key and **Description** boxes blank. In the **Store macro in:** box, select **This Workbook**. Click **OK**.

3. In the **Home** tab, locate the **Cells** group, click the **Format** dropdown, and select **Row Height.**

4. In the **Row Height** dialog box, enter **30**, and click **OK**.

5. In the **Home** tab, locate the **Font** group, and change the Font Size drop down to **12**.

6. In the **View** tab, locate the **Macros** group, select the **Macros** drop down, and click **Stop Recording**.

7. Select the range **A3:G9**. In the view tab, locate the **Macros** group, and click **Macros**. Run the macro **Height**.

Ex1_Q25.

1. In the **View** tab, locate the **Macros** group, click the **Macros** drop down, and select **Record Macro...**

2. In the **Macro name** field, enter **Formatting**. in the **Store macro in:** drop down, select **This Workbook**. Leave all other settings as the default, and click **OK**.

3. In the **Home** tab, locate the **number** group, and select **Currency** from the dropdown.

4. In the **Home** tab, locate the **Styles** group, and select the **Conditional Formatting** dropdown.

5. Select **Data Bars**, and click **Blue Data Bar** in the **Gradient** section.

6. In the **View** tab, locate the **Macros** group, click the **Macros** dropdown, and click **Stop Recording**.

7. Select the cell range **B4:G9**. In the **View** tab, locate the **Macros** group, click the **Macros** button, and **Run** the macro named **Formatting**.

Ex1_Q26.

If you do not have the Developer tab, you will need it:

1. Click on the **File** tab, select **Options**, and select the **Customize Ribbon** tab.

2. Make sure that **Developer** is checked in the **Main Tabs** section. Click **OK**

3. In the **Family Budget** worksheet, in the **Developer** tab, go to the **Controls** group, click the **Insert** drop down and select **Button (Form Control)**.

4. Click and drag over 1 to 2 open cells, in the **Assign Macro** window click **Set_Data_Bars** and click **OK**.

5. Click into the button to rename it, and enter **Set Data Bars**.

6. Click off the button, and then click the button to run it.

Ex1_Q27.

1. In the **Sales Orders** worksheet, in cell **H4**, right click on the **Spin Button** and click **Format Control**

2. In the **Format Control** window, go to the **Control** tab, in the **Minimum value** field enter **1** in the **Maximum value** field enter **100** and in the **Incremental change** field enter **1**.

3. Click **OK**.

Ex1_Q28.

If you do not have the Developer tab, you will need it:

1. Click on the **File** tab, select **Options**, and select the **Customize Ribbon** tab.

2. Make sure that **Developer** is checked in the **Main Tabs** section. Click **OK**

3. In the **Sale Orders** worksheet, click into the table, in the **Developer** tab, go to the **XML** group and click **Map Properties**.

4. In the **XML Map Properties** window, in the **Name** field enter **NewOrders**, under the **Data formatting and layout** section check the **Adjust column width** box.

5. Under the **When refreshing or importing data** section check the **Overwrite existing data with new data** radio button and click **OK**.

6. In the **Developer** tab, go to the **XML** group, and click **Export**.

7. Locate your GMetrixTemplates folder inside your Documents folder. In the file name enter **NewOrdersXML** and set the type to **XML Files (*.xml)** and click **Export**.

Ex1_Q29.

1. In the **File** tab, in the **Info** section, click on the drop down for **Properties** in the right hand column.

2. Click **Advanced Properties**, and choose the **Custom** tab

3. In **Name:** type **Completed**. In the drop down for **Type:** choose **Yes or No**. In **Value:** click **No**.

4. Click **Add**

5. Click **OK**

EXERCISE 2 QUESTIONS

Ex2_Q1.

Save the workbook as a template named **EmployeeReview** in any folder in your documents folder.

Notes:

_____

_____

_____

_____

_____

Ex2_Q2.

Require a password to open the current workbook using the password **ReviewHR9**

Notes:

_____

_____

_____

_____

_____

Ex2_Q3.

Protect the Employee Data worksheet with the password **ED2HR** (Leave all other settings as Default.)

Notes:

_____

_____

_____

_____

_____

_____

Ex2_Q4.

Track all changes that have ever been made by any user on this shared document, only highlight changes when lasted saved. (Leave all other settings as Default.)

Ex2_Q5.

Merge the Ex2_Q1.xlsx worksheets with the current workbook.

Notes:

_____

_____

_____

_____

_____

Ex2_Q6.

In the **Business Trip Budget** worksheet, use the **Trace Precedents** for cell **G18** to determine the problem, and fix the formula.

Notes:

_____

_____

_____

_____

_____

Ex2_Q7.

Configure Excel Formulas to have the R1C1 reference style and enable Error Checking using the colour Blue.

Notes:

_____

_____

_____

_____

_____

Ex2_Q8.

In the Yearly Timesheet worksheet, add watches to cells I4, K4 and M4.

Ex2_Q9.

Provide the option for Excel to highlight formulas that refer to empty cells in the **Error checking rules**.

Notes:

_____

_____

_____

_____

_____

_____

Ex2_Q10.

In the **Startup Purchases** worksheet, using the **SUMIF** formula in the **Total Amount** Paid Off (**cell D22**), use the "**Paid?**" range data to compute the total of paid items.

Notes:

_____

_____

_____

_____

_____

_____

Ex2_Q11.

In the **Startup Expenses** worksheet, in cell **G11** do a **COUNTIF** for all the Totals below (**C11:C28**) to find out how many are greater than **125,000**

Notes:

_____

_____

_____

_____

_____

Ex2_Q12.

In the **Invoice Tracker** worksheet, under **Outstanding Invoices** (in cell **C23**) do a **COUNTIFS** for each client to find out how many still need to make payments on their invoices.

Notes:

_____

_____

_____

_____

_____

Ex2_Q13.

In the **Calculations** worksheet, in cell **F22** use the **COUNTIF** formula to find out how many employees are in the **R&D** Department.

Notes:

_____

_____

_____

_____

_____

Ex2_Q14.

In the **Calculations** worksheet, in cell **H18** use the **SUMIF** formula to find out how many **Total Sick Days** are in the **Finance Department**.

Notes:

_____

_____

_____

_____

_____

Ex2_Q15.

In the **Business Trip Budget** worksheet, use the **Evaluate Formula** tool to correct the error in **G19** and simplify and correct the complex formula

Ex2_Q16.

In the **Dashboard** worksheet, create a **VLOOKUP** function in cell **N39** that finds the Bonus (Column 4) in the **Employee Data** worksheet for the Employee in **N35** in the **Dashboard** worksheet.

Notes:

_____

_____

_____

_____

_____

_____

Ex2_Q17.

In the **Dashboard** worksheet, add a **Linear Forecast** trendline to the **Number of Employees by Year** chart.

Notes:

_____

_____

_____

_____

Ex2_Q18.

In the **Dashboard** worksheet, fix the **Salary Distribution** chart to select the **Bonus** data from the **Employee Data** worksheet.

Notes:

_____

_____

_____

_____

_____

Ex2_Q19.

In the **Yearly Charts** worksheet, change the **January** chart to **Style 4**. Save the chart as a **chart template** with the name **TimecardChart** in the **GTotalsTemplates** folder located in your documents folder.

Notes:

_____

_____

_____

_____

_____

Ex2_Q20.

Using the **Goal Seek Data Tool** set your **Trip Budget** for **Company (B23)** to **$15,000** to find out how many people are able to go on the business trip.

Notes:

_____

_____

_____

_____

_____

Ex2_Q21.

Create and show a scenario named **<u>Less</u>** that only gives **half** of what the **budget** had for **Entertainment** in cell **C15**. Create a Scenario Summary of the **Less Scenario.**

Notes:

_____

_____

_____

_____

_____

Ex2_Q22.

In the **Employee Data Pivot Chart** worksheet, insert slicers for **Full Name**, **Salary** and **Department**.

Notes:

_____

_____

_____

_____

_____

_____

Ex2_Q23.

In the **Invoice Tracker worksheet, insert a PivotTable beneath the data in cell E22 and shows the Invoice # and Outstanding data. Use the data in range B4:J17**

Notes:

_____

_____

_____

_____

_____

Ex2_Q24.

In the **Employee Data Pivot Chart** worksheet, edit the **PivotChart**, and place the **Full Name** field into the **Axis (Categories)** group and the **Performance Score** into the **Values** group

Notes:

_____

_____

_____

_____

_____

Ex2_Q25.

In the **Invoice Tracker** worksheet, insert a **PivotTable** for cell range **B4:J17** into a new sheet that displays **Customer Name** and **Amount**. Accept all other defaults

Notes:

_____

_____

_____

_____

_____

Ex2_Q26.

In the **Invoice Tracker** worksheet, create a macro that sets the **Width** of all the columns to be **25**. Name the macro **ColumnWidth**, and store it in only this workbook (Leave all other settings as default settings.) and stop recording the Macro

Notes:

_____

_____

_____

_____

_____

_____

Ex2_Q27.

In the **Invoice Tracker** worksheet, assign the **Change_Colour** macro to the button **Change Table Colour** and click the button to run the Macro

Notes:

_____

_____

_____

_____

_____

_____

Ex2_Q28.

In the **Startup Expenses** worksheet, create a **Spin Button** in cell **F8:F9** so that it changes the values in cell **F7** to numbers 1 - 100 in increments of 1. (Note: Accept all other default settings.)

Notes:

_____

_____

_____

_____

_____

Ex2_Q29.

In the **Dashboard** worksheet, link the **Form Control** above the **Employee Information** table to the **Employee Data** worksheet to the data under the <u>first column</u> heading and have the cell link be at **P34** on the **Dashboard** worksheet.

Notes:

_____

_____

_____

_____

_____

EXERCISE 2: ANSWERS

Ex2_Q1.

1. In the **File** tab, click **Save As**.

2. In the **Save As** dialog window, locate your PureSoftwareTemplate folder in your documents folder, go to the **Save as type** drop down and select **Excel Template (.xltx)**.

3. Ensure that you are still in the PureSoftwareTemplate folder

4. In the **File name** field enter **EmployeeReview** and click **Save**.

Ex2_Q2.

1. Click on File tab. On the Info tab, select the Protect Workbook button and click **Encrypt with Password**.

2. In the dialog window enter the password **ReviewHR9** and click **OK**.

Ex2_Q3.

1. In the **Employee Data** worksheet, go to the **Review** tab, in the **Changes** group click **Protect S**heet.

2. In the **Protect Sheet** dialog window, in the **Password to unprotect sheet** field enter **ED2HR** and click **OK**.

Ex2_Q4.

1. In the **Employee Data** worksheet, in the **Review** tab, go to the **Changes** group, select the **Track Changes** drop down and click **Highlight Changes**.

2. In the **Highlight Changes** dialog window, click **Track changes while editing**. Set the **When** drop down to **Since I Last Saved**

3. Click the **Who** checkbox and set the drop down to **Everyone** and click **OK**.

Ex2_Q5.

1. In the **File** tab, click **Open** and then computer. Locate the **PureTrainingTemplate** folder in your documents folder. Open **Ex2_Q1.xlsx**.

2. In **Ex2_Q1.xlsx** right click on the **Invoice Tracker** worksheet, and click **Move or Copy**.

3. In the **Move or Copy** dialog window, select the **To book** drop down and select **Ex2_Q5.xlsx**. In the **Before sheet** field select **Yearly Timesheet** and click **OK**.

Ex2_Q6.

1. In the **Business Trip Budget** worksheet, select cell **G18**.

2. In the **Formulas** tab, go to the **Formula Auditing** group and click **Trace Precedents**.

3. You will see that it is skipping cell G13. Select cells **G18**, in the **Home** tab, go to the **Editing** group and click the **AutoSum** drop down and select **Sum** and press Enter

Ex2_Q7.

1. In the **File** tab, click **Options**.

2. In the **Excel Options** window, select the **Formulas** tab, in the **Working with formulas** section check **R1C1 reference style**.

3. In the Error Checking section check **Enable background error checking**. In the colour drop down select **Blue** and click **OK**.

Ex2_Q8.

1. In the **Yearly Timesheet** worksheet, in the **Formulas** tab, go to the **Formula Auditing** group and click **Watch Window**.

2. In the **Watch Window** dialog window, click **Add Watch**.

3. Select cell **I4** and click **Add**.

4. Repeat steps 2 and 4 for cells **K4** and **M4**.

Ex2_Q9.

1. In the **File** tab, click **Options**.

2. In the **Excel Options** window, in the **Formulas** tab, go to the **Error checking rules** section and check **Formulas referring to empty cells** and click **OK**.

Ex2_Q10.

1. In the **Startup Purchases** worksheet, select cell **C22**. In the **Formulas** tab, go to the **Function Library** group and click **Insert Function**.

2. In the **Insert Function** window, search for **SUMIF** and click **GO**. Select **SUMIF** from the window below and click **OK**.

3. In the **Function Arguments** window, in the **Range** field select cells **D4:D20**.

4. In the **Criteria** field enter **Yes** and for the **Sum_range** field select the data in cells **C4:C20** and click **OK**.

Ex2_Q11.

1. In the **Startup Expenses** worksheet, select cell **G11**. In the **Formulas** tab, go to the **Function Library** group and click **Insert Function**.

2. In the **Insert Function** window, search for **COUNTIF** and click **GO**. Select **COUNTIF** from the window below and click **OK**.

3. In the **Function Arguments** window, in the **Range** field select cells **G15:G28**.

4. In the **Criteria** field enter **>125000** and click **OK**.

Ex2_Q12.

1. In the **Invoice Tracker** worksheet, select cells **C23:C26**. In the **Formulas** tab, go to the **Function Library** group and click **Insert Function**.

2. In the **Insert Function** window, in the **Search for Function** text box, enter **COUNTIFS** and click **GO**. Select **COUNTIFS** in the window below and click **OK**.

3. In the **Function Arguments** window, for the **Criteria_range1** field select cells **J4:J17** and in the **Criteria1** field enter **>0**.

4. In the **Criteria_range2** field select cells **E4:E17** and in the **Criteria2** field select cell **B23:B26** and click **OK**.

Ex2_Q13.

1. In the **Calculations** worksheet, select cell **F22**. In the **Formulas** tab, go to the **Function Library** and click **Insert Function**.

2. In the **Insert Function** window, search for **COUNTIF** and click **GO**. In the window select **COUNTIF** and click **OK**.

3. In the **Function Arguments** window, in the **Range** field select the data in the **Employee Data** worksheet from **F3:F98**. In the **Criteria** field select cell **A22 (R&D)** in the **Calculations** worksheet and click **OK**.

Ex2_Q14.

1. In the **Calculations** worksheet, select cell **H18**. In the **Formulas** tab, go to the **Function Library** and click **Insert Function**.

2. In the **Insert Function** window, search for **SUMIF** and click **GO**. In the window select **SUMIF** and click **OK**.

3. In the **Function Arguments** window, in the **Range** field select the data in the **Employee Data** worksheet from cells **F3:F98**. In the **Criteria** field select cell **A18** in the **Calculations** worksheet, in the **Sum range** field select data from the **Employee Data** worksheet from cells **G3:G98** and click **OK**.

Ex2_Q15.

1. In the **Business Trip Budget** worksheet, select cell **G19**, in the **Formulas** tab, go to the **Formula Auditing** group and click **Evaluate Formula**.

2. In the **Evaluate Formula** window, click **Evaluate** to go through the steps of the formula until it returns to the first step, then click **Close**. (Look closely at what the formula is doing and how to correct it.)

3. In cell **G19** enter the formula **=B4-G18**.

Ex2_Q16.

1. In the **Dashboard** worksheet, select cell **N39**. In the **Formulas** tab, go to the **Function Library** and click **Insert Function**.

2. In the **Insert Function** window, search for **VLOOKUP** and click **GO**. In the window select **VLOOKUP** and click **OK**.

3. In the **Function Arguments** window, in the **Lookup_value** field select the data in the cell **N35**.

4. In the **Table_array** field select the data in the Employee Data worksheet cell **A3:H98**.

5. In the **Col_index_num** enter <u>4</u>. In the Range_lookup, enter **FALSE** and click **OK**.

Ex2_Q17.

1. In the **Dashboard** worksheet, select the **Number of Employees by Year** chart.

2. Click the **chart elements** button that appears at the top right of the chart. Select the **Trendline** drop down and click **linear forecast**.

Ex2_Q18.

1. In the **Dashboard** worksheet, select the **Salary Distribution** chart.

2. In the **Design** tab, go to the **Data** group and click **Select Data**.

3. In the **Select Data Source** window, select the data from **D3:D98** and click **OK**.

Ex2_Q19.

1. In the **Yearly Charts** worksheet, select the **January** chart. In the **Design** tab, go to the **Chart Styles** group and select **Style 4**.

2. Right click in the Yearly Charts worksheets and select the **Save As Template**

3. In the **Save Chart Template** window, locate the GTotalTemplates folder located in your documents folder. In the **File name** field enter **TimecardChart** and click **Save**.

Ex2_Q20.

1. In the **Business Trip Budget** worksheet, select cell **B23**. In the **Data** tab, go to the **Data Tools** group, select the **What-If Analysis** drop down and click **Goal Seek**.

2. In the **Goal Seek** window, set the Set cell field as **B23**, set the To value field to 15000 and the By changing cell field to **B22** and click **OK** twice.

Ex2_Q21.

1. In the **Data** tab, go to the **Data Tools** group, select the **What-If Analysis** drop down and click **Scenario Manager**.

2. In the **Scenario Manager** window, click **Add**. In the **Scenario name** field enter **Less**. Set the Changing cells to **C15** and click **OK**.

3. In the Scenario Values window set the value to **65** and click **OK**.

4. Select the Result cells (**G18:G19**)

5. In the **Scenario Manager**, highlight the **Less** Scenario and click **Summary**

In the **Scenario Summary** window click **OK**

Ex2_Q22.

1. In the **Employee Data Pivot Chart** worksheet, highlight the **PivotTable**.

2. Click the Insert tab.

3. In the **Filter** group click **Slicer**

2. In the **Insert Slicers** window, click **Full Name**, **Salary** and **Department** and click **OK**.

Ex2_Q23.

1. In the **Invoice Tracker** worksheet, in the **Insert** tab, locate the **Tables** group, and click **PivotTable**

2. In the Create **PivotTable** window, for **select a table or range** select the cells **B4:J17** and under the **Choose where...** section click Existing Worksheet. In the Location field select **E22** and click **OK**.

3. Highlight the **PivotTable** and in the **PivotTable Fields** window select **Invoice #** and **Outstanding**.

Ex2_Q24.

1. In the **Employee Data Pivot Chart** worksheet, highlight the **PivotChart**.

2. In the **PivotChart Fields** window, drag **Full Name** to the **Axis (Categories)** group below and the **Performance Score** to the **Values** group below.

Ex2_Q25.

In the **Invoice Tracker** worksheet, insert a **PivotTable** for cell range **B4:J17** into a new sheet that displays **Customer Name** and **Amount**. Accept all other defaults

1. In the **Invoice Tracker** worksheet select the, in the **Insert** tab, go to the **Tables** group, select the **PivotTable** drop down and click **PivotTable**.

2. In the **Create PivotTable** window, in the select a table or range select the cells **B4:J17** and under the Choose where... section click **New Worksheet** and click **OK**.

3. Highlight the PivotTable and in the **PivotTable Field List** window select **Customer Name** and **Amount**.

Ex2_Q26.

1. In the **Invoice Tracker** worksheet, in the **Developer** tab, go to the **Code** group, and click **Record Macro**.

2. In the **Record Macro** dialog window in the **Macro name** field enter **ColumnWidth** and click **OK**.

3. Select columns B to J. Right-click on any of the column's while the columns are selected and click **Column Width**.

4. In the **Column Width** dialog window, enter 25 and click **OK**.

5. In the **Developer** tab, go to the **Code** group and click **Stop Recording**.

Ex2_Q27.

1. In the **Invoice Tracker** worksheet, right click on the **Change Table Colour** button below the table and click **Assign Macro...**

2. In the **Assign Macro** dialog window, select the **Change Colour** macro from the list and click **OK**. Click out of the **Change Table Colour** button, so it is no longer selected.

3. Click the **Change Table Colour** button.

Ex2_Q28.

1. In the **Startup Expenses** worksheet, in the **Developer** tab, go to the **Controls** group, in the **Insert** dropdown select **Spin Button**.

2. Draw the Spin Button in top of cell **F8** to the bottom right of **F9**. Right click on the Spin Button and select **Format Control**.

3. In the **Format Control** dialog window set the **Minimum value** to 1 and **Maximum value** to 100. Set the Cell link to cell F7 and click **OK**.

Ex2_Q29.

1. In the **Dashboard** worksheet, right click on the **Form Control** above the **Employee Information** table and click **Format Control**.

2. In the **Format Object** dialog window, in the **Control** tab, enter your cursor into the **Input Range** field and select the **Employee Data** worksheet, highlight all the data from cell **A3:A98.**

3. In the **Format Object** dialog window, click into the **Cell link** field and in the **Dashboard** worksheet select cell **P34** and click **OK.**

EXERCISE 3: QUESTIONS & ANSWERS

Ex3_Q1.

Protect the structure of the workbook.

1. Choose **Review** ⇨ **Changes** ⇨ **Protect Workbook**
2. In the Protect Workbook dialog box, select the **Structure** option
3. (Optional) Provide a password.

Notes:

To unprotect the workbook, repeat the process and untick the **Structure** option and click **Cancel.**

_____

_____

_____

_____

Ex3_Q2.

Make the **Loan Payment** worksheet "VeryHidden" so that you cannot unhide it in the normal way.

1. Activate the **Loan Payment** worksheet ⇨ Chose **Developer** ⇨ **Controls** ⇨ **Properties**
2. In the **Properties** dialog box, select the Visible property and choose **2-SheetVeryHidden.**

Notes:

To unhide a sheet that is VeryHidden, Press Alt-F11 to activate the Visual Basic editor. Locate the workbook in the Projects window and select the name of the sheet that is VeryHidden. Press F4 to display the Properties dialog box, then change the Visible property back to 1-SheetVisible.

• You cannot hide the last and only sheet in a workbook.

_____

_____

_____

_____

Ex3_Q3.

On the **Business Trip Budget** worksheet, provide a **Watch Window** for cells **G18** and **G19.**

1. On the **Business Trip Budget** worksheet, Click the **Formula** tab
2. In the **Formula Auditing** group click **Watch Window**
3. Select cells **G18** and **G19**
4. On the **Watch Window** dialog box, click **Add Watch.**
5. On the **Add Watch** dialog box click the **Add** button.

Notes:

_____

_____

_____

_____

Ex3_Q4.

Apply the **Accounting** formatting to cells **B4:F8** in all the four worksheets in a **group mode** (i.e. apply the format to all the sheets at once, not one by one).

1. Activate the first (**Totals**) sheet
2. Select the range **B4:F8**
3. Press **Shift** and click the **Manufacture** sheet tab (the last sheet)
4. Click the **Home** tab and then click the **Number** group dialog launcher
5. Select **Accounting** and click **OK**
6. Right-click any of the grouped sheets and select **Ungroup sheets**

Ex3_Q5.

On the **Totals** worksheet, change the shape of the rectangular comments box in cell **F8** to a different shape of your choice. Hint: First you need to add a command to the Quick Access toolbar:

1. Right-click on the Quick Access toolbar and choose **Customize Quick Access Toolbar**
2. From the **Choose Command from** drop-down list, select **Drawing Tools | Format Tab**
3. From the list on the left, select **Change Shape**, and then click **Add**, then click **OK.**
4. Make the comment box visible.
5. Press the **Ctrl** key and click the rectangular **Comment** box.
6. Click the **Change Shape** button on the **Quick Access** toolbar and choose a new shape for the comment.

_____

_____

_____

_____

_____

Ex3_Q6

Print the **Totals** worksheet together with its comments. The comments should appear on a separate page at the end of the sheet printout.

Click the dialog box launcher (⧉) in the **Page Layout** ⇨ **Page Setup** group.

1. In the **Page Setup** dialog box, click the **Sheet** tab.
2. In the **Comments** textbox select **At End of Sheet**, and click **OK.**

Ex3_Q7.

In the **House Sales** worksheet sort the table data by: **Agent (A-Z)**, then by **Area (Z-A)** and finally by **List Price (smallest to largest)**

1. Click any cell within the data cells.
2. In the **Editing** group on the **Home** tab, click on the **Sort & Filter** tab.
3. Select **Custom Sort** to open the **Custom Sort** dialog box
4. In the **Sort by** drop-down list select **Agent,** In the **Sort On** drop-down, select **Value,** and in **the Order** drop-down select **A-Z.** Click **Add Level.**

5. In the **Sort by** drop-down list select **Area,** In the **Sort On** drop-down, select **Value,** and in **the Order** drop-down select **Z-A**. Click **Add Level**.
6. In the **Sort by** drop-down list select **List Price,** In the **Sort On** drop-down, select **Value,** and in **the Order** drop-down select **Smallest to Largest**.

Notes:

_____

_____

_____

_____

Ex3_Q8.

In the **House Sales** worksheet, using Slicers, filter the table data to show only records for the Agent called **Adams** in the **Central** Area.

1. Click any cell in the table.
2. In the **Filters** group on the **Insert** tab, click **Slicer.**
3. Check the **Agent** and **Area** boxes and click **OK**
4. On the **Agent** slicer click **Adams**, and click **Central** on the **Area** slicer

Notes:

1. To remove the filter click on the Clear Filter icon or use Alt + C

2. To delete the slicer, activate it and press Delete

_____

_____

_____

_____

Ex3_Q9.

In addition to Excel's **XLStart** folder, use the "**C:\Pure Training**" folder, as an alternate Startup folder.

1. Choose **File** ⇨ **Options** and select the **Advanced** tab.
2. Scroll down to the **General** section and enter a new folder name (in this case "**C:\Pure Training**") in the **At Startup, open all files in** textbox.

Notes: 1

Excel will attempt to open all files (e.g. *.docx) that are stored in this folder. Make sure only the Excel file that you wish to open at startup is stored in the folder

Ex3_Q10.

Protect only the formula cells on Sheet1 (Leave nonformula cells unprotected).

1. Choose **Home** ⇨ **Editing** Find & Select ⇨ **Go to Special**.
2. Select **Constants** and click **OK**. All nonformula cells are selected
3. Press **Ctrl + 1** to open the **Format Cell** dialog box
4. Select the **Protection** tab
5. Remove the check mark from the **Locked** checkbox, and click **Ok**.
6. Choose **Review** ⇨ **Changes** ⇨ Protect Sheet
7. (Optional) Specify a password and click **OK**

Notes:

_____

_____

_____

Ex3_Q11.

In Sheet1 print only range **A11:H23 (yellow highlight)**.

1. In **Sheet1**, select range **A11:H23**.
2. On the Ribbon click **File** ⇨ **Print**.
3. In the Print dialog box, under **Settings**, click the drop-down arrow for the **Print Active Sheets** option and click the **Print Selection** option.

Notes:

_____

_____

_____

Ex3_Q12.

On the Customer Contact Details sheet, insert **FIRST PAGE HEADER** in the first page header only. Insert **FIRST PAGE FOOTER** in the first page footer only. Insert **ODD PAGE HEADER** in all odd page headers and **ODD PAGE FOOTER** in all odd page footers. Insert **EVEN PAGE HEADER** in all even page headers, then insert **EVEN PAGE FOOTER** in all even page footers.

1. On the Ribbon, click **View** ⇨ **Workbook View** ⇨ **Page Layout**
2. Click in the box containing the text "**Click to Add Header**"
3. Click the **DESIGN** tab under **Header & Footer Tools**.
4. In the **Options** group, check the check boxes for **Different First Page** and **Different Odd and Even Pages.**
5. Type **FIRST PAGE HEADER** in the header box for the first page.
6. Type **FIRST PAGE FOOTER** in the footer box for the first page.
7. On the header and footer boxes for pages 1 and 2 type the appropriate text.

Notes:

_____

_____

_____

_____

Ex3_Q13.

On the **Customer Contact Details** worksheet, configure **Page Setup** for "**Landscape**" orientation and set **Page Size** to **B5**. Apply the configuration to **Sheet1** worksheet.

1. Activate the **Customer Contact Details** worksheet (source).
2. Select the target sheet (the new sheet). Do a Ctrl + click to activate both sheets.
3. Click the dialog box launcher in the lower right corner of the **Page Layout Page Setup** group.
4. When the dialog box appears, click **OK** and close it.
5. Ungroup the sheet by right-clicking any selected sheet and choosing **Ungroup Sheets** from the shortcut menu.

Notes:

_____

_____

_____

_____

Ex3_Q14.

Set up the **Customer Contact Details** sheet so that the SmartArt Graphic (with the text "**Do not Print**") does not print when the worksheet is printed.

1. Right-click the object and choose **Format Shape**
2. In the **Format** dialog box, click the **Size & Properties** icon
3. Expand the **Properties** section of the dialog box
4. Remove the check mark for **Print Object**

Notes:

_____

_____

_____

_____

Ex3_Q15.

Create a custom view named "**Customer Contact Details No1**" for the **Customer Contact Details** sheet. Accept all default options

1. Choose **View** ⇨ **Workbook View** ⇨ **Custom Views**. The Custom Views dialog box appears.
2. Click the Add button.
3. On the Add View dialog box type **Customer Contact Details No1** in the **Name** box.

Notes:

1. You will normally create different views (with different settings for different requirements) for the same worksheet.

2. The Custom View command is disabled if ANY sheet in the workbook has a table.
3. When you are ready to print, just select the appropriate view (e.g. one with correct print margins etc.)

Ex3_Q16.

The data in range **B3:D14** is a table called **Table1**. Without resorting to using any Excel formula, show the **sum** of the **Projected** column and the **Standard Deviation** of the data in the **Actual** column (include a **Total** row in the table).

1. Click any cell in the table (**Table1**).
2. Under **Table Tools**, click **Design.**
3. In the **Table Style Options** group, put a check mark in the **Total Row** check box.
4. Click the cell in the **Total** row in the Projected column (cell **C15**). In the drop-down list select **SUM.**
5. 5.   Click the cell in the **Total** row in the **Actual** column (cell **D15**). In the drop-down list select **StdDev.**

Notes:

Ex3_Q17.

On the **Accounts** sheet in cell **B17**, use the **DSUM** function to calculate the total account balance for all **Open** accounts that have rates greater than 2 percent.

Figure Ex3_Q17

1. Create a table as shown above on the **Account** sheet
2. Create this formula in cell **B17**: **=DSUM (A5:D15,"Balance", A2:D3)**

Notes:

1. DSUM syntax: DSUM (Database, Field, Criteria range)
2. Database (range) is: A5:D15
3. Target field for calculation is: "Balance"

4. Criteria range is: A2:D3 (this range can be placed anywhere on the sheet)

Ex3_Q18.

In the **Data** worksheet, use the **ROW** and **INDIRECT** functions to calculate the total of the five largest values in range **A1:A25**.

1. Select any empty cell in the data sheet
2. Use this formula: **={SUM(LARGE(A1:A25, ROW(INDIRECT("1:5"))))}**

Notes:

1. DO NOT type the curly brackets ({})
2. After typing the formula, press Shift+Ctrl+ENTER (DO NOT press only the ENTER key)
3. The combination of the ROW and INDIRECT functions produces the array {1,2,3,4,5}
4. So in effect the formula becomes: SUM(LARGE (A1:A25,{1,2,3,4,5}))
5. Read on the LARGE, ROW and INDIRECT functions

Ex3_Q19.

In cell **B3** on the **Tax Rate** sheet, use the **VLOOKUP** function to retrieve the value of the **Tax Rate** for an income of **$55,000**.

1. In cell **B3** insert this formula: **=VLOOKUP(55000,D2:F7,3)**

Notes:

1. Syntax: VLOOKUP (lookup_value, table_array, col_index_num [,range_lookup]
2. If an exact match is not found in the first column of the lookup table, VLOOKUP uses the next largest value that is less than the lookup value.

Ex3_Q20.

Make the necessary adjustment on the **Chart** worksheet so that only **Chart1** and the data should appear when the sheet is printed. **Chart2** should not be printed.

1. Access the **Format Chart Area** task pane for **Chart2** (Double-click the **Chart Area** for **Chart2**).
2. Select the **Property & Size** icon.
3. 3. Expand the **Properties** section and clear the **Print** check box.

Notes:

Ex3_Q21.

On **Sheet1**, hide (**NOT** delete) the data series for **Precipitation** from the **Weather Summary** chart.

1. Activate the chart and click **Chart Filter** button on the right.
2. Remove the check mark from the data series for **Precipitation**

Notes:

_____

_____

_____

_____

Ex3_Q22.

On the **Combo Chart** sheet, create a **combination chart** for the two data series (**Column chart** for the **Avg. Temp** series and **Line chart** for the **Precipitation** series).

Make the Precipitation data series the Secondary Axis.

1. Select any cell in the data area
2. Choose **Insert** ⇨ Charts ⇨ **Recommended Charts**.
3. Select the **All Charts** tab.
4. In the list of chart types, click **Combo**.
5. For the **Avg. Temp** series, specify **Clustered Column** as the chart type
6. For the **Precipitation** series, specify **Line** as the chart type and click the **Secondary Axis** check box.
7. Click **OK** to insert the chart

Notes:

Ex3_Q23.

On the **nonnumeric** sheet, format only the text entries (cells containing text) **bold.** All cells containing numbers should not be formatted.

1. Select the range **A1:B10** and ensure that cell **A1** is the active cell.
2. Choose **Home** ⇨ **Styles** ⇨ **Conditional Formatting** ⇨ **New Rule**.
3. Click the **Use Formula to Determine Which Cells to Format** rule type.
4. Enter the following formula in the Formula box: **=ISTEXT(A1).**

5. Click the **Format** button.
6. From the **Font** tab, select **Bold.**
7. Click **OK** to return to the **New Formatting Rule** dialog box
8. Click **OK** to close the New **Formatting Rule** dialog box

Notes:

1. If the formula that is entered into the conditional formatting dialog box contains a cell reference, that reference is considered a relative reference, based on the upper-left cell in the selected range.

_____

_____

_____

_____

Ex3_Q24.

On the **Custom Format** sheet, using the **Today ()** function enter today's date in cell **A1** in the format "**mm/dd/yyyy**" or "**dd/mm/yyyy**". Format the cell to read, for example, **August 03, 2015 (Monday)** in **Red** text

Notes:

1. In cell **A1** enter: =**Today()**
2. Click the dialog box launcher of the **Home** ⇨ **Font** tab
3. Click the **Number** tab. In the **Category** list select the **Custom** option
4. In the **Type** box enter the following format: **[RED]mmmm dd, yyyy (dddd)**

_____

** **Open the Custom Format Example sheet to see examples of custom formatting.**

_____

_____

_____

Ex3_Q25.

Apply the **General** format as the <u>default</u> format for the workbook.

Notes:

1. Select the **Home** tab ⇨ **Style** ⇨ **Cell Style** drop-down.

2. Right-click the **Normal** style ⇨ **Modify**. Select the **General** format. Click **OK**.

_____

_____

_____

_____

Ex3_Q26.

On the **West Companies** sheet, modify the existing **Conditional Formatting** rule to remove the values from then **2015 Sales** column and show only the data bars.

Notes:

1. Click **Home** ⇨ **Styles** ⇨ **Conditional Formatting** ⇨ **Manage Rules**
2. On the **Show format rule for** drop-down box select "**This Worksheet**"
3. Activate the **Data Bar** rule and click **Edit Rule...**
4. Click the **Show bar only** text box

Ex3_Q27.

On the **Feb_Humidity** sheet, highlight (using Red colour) all humidity values that are **less** than their corresponding **Jan_Humidity** values.

1. Select the humidity values on the **Feb Humidity** sheet (**B2:H21**).
2. Click **Home** ⇨ **Styles** ⇨ **Conditional Formatting** drop-down
3. Select the **Manage Rules...** option
4. On the **Conditional Formatting Rules Manager** dialog box, click the **New Rule** tab.
5. Select the **Use a formula to determine which cells to format** option.
6. In the **Format values where this formula is true** text box, type the following formula: **B2< Jan_Humidity!B2**
7. Click the Format tab and in the Colour drop-down select Red

Note: If you select the cells for the formula instead of typing them in, excel by default will add the $ signs for absolute references. In that case manually delete the $ signs

Ex3_Q28.

In the **Auto Fill** sheet, Create an **Auto Fill** using the cities in cells **A3:A11**. Type **Sydney** in cell **C3** and drag the **Fill handler** to auto-fill cells **C4:C11** with the rest of the cities (just as in cells **A3:A11**).

Notes:

1. Click **File** ⇨ **Options** ⇨ **Advanced**.
2. Scroll down and click the **Edit Custom List** button.
3. In the **List entries** list box enter the cities (**Sydney...Newcastle**), separated by commas (,).
4. Click **Add** and then click **OK.**
5. In the **Auto Fill** sheet, select cell **C3**, enter **Sydney.**
6. Drag down to fill the cells.

Ex3_Q29.

In the Status Chart worksheet, change the chart layout to Layout 1, change the chart title to Employment History and change the chart style to Style 9. Save the chart as a chart template to the PureSoftwareTemplate folder in your documents folder and with the name EmploymentChart

Notes:

1. Select the Status Chart worksheet. On this worksheet, select the chart
2. Click Chart Tools Design Chart Layouts group and click the Quick Layout dropdown, and select Layout 1
3. Click on Chart Title and type "Employment History"
4. In the Chart Tools Design tab, locate the Chart Styles group and click the drop down. Select Style 9
5. Right click the chart and click Save as Template. Navigate to the PureSoftwareTemplate folder in your documents folder, name the template EmploymentChart and click Save.

Ex3_Q30.

Using a named formula called "**Address**", the **INDEX** function and the **MATCH** function, provide a means to retrieve the address into cell **G3** for a name entered in cell **G1**. Use one of the names in the **A3:A10** range. Ensure that no error message is shown if the name does not exist in the list. If the name does not exist, the address cell (**G3**) must be blank.

1. Click **Formula** ⇨ **Define Names** ⇨ **Define Name**
2. In the **New Name** dialog box, enter "**Address**" into the **Name** textbox
3. In the "**Refers to:**" textbox, enter:
   =IFERROR (INDEX($A$3:$B$10, MATCH($G$1,$A$3:$A$10,0),2),"")

4. Click **OK**
5. In cell **G3** enter the formula "**=Address**"

EXERCISE 4: QUESTIONS & ANSWERS

Ex4_Q1.

Use the data in cells **A3:A10** as a drop-down list for cell **G1**. Then in cell **G3**, write a **VLOOKUP** function to show the address of a name selected from the drop-down list in cell **G1**.

1. Click in cell **G1**.
2. Click **Data** ⇨ **Data Tools**. Click the drop-down arrow for the **Data Validation** tab.
3. In the **Data validation** dialog box, in the **Allow:** drop-down, select **List**
4. Click in the Source textbox and highlight cells **A3:A10**. Click **OK.**
5. Enter this formula in cell G3: "**=VLOOKUP(G1, A3:B10, 2, FALSE)**"

Ex4_Q2.

** Use ONLY The INDEX, MATCH, VLOOKUP and DOLLAR functions for the following question:

The "**Dollar, Match, VLOOKUP & Index**" Worksheet has 3 option buttons for mailing types and costs. Cell **B2** is a linked cell for the option buttons. Using the data area (range **A7:C9**), construct a formula that will display the following information in cell **A12**:

a. When you select **Option 1 (Air Mail)**, cell **A12** should read: "**Cost of Using Air Mail is $124.78**"
b. When you select **Option 2 (Courier)**, cell **A12** should read: "**Cost of Using Courier is $450**"
c. When you select **Option 3 (Surface Mail)** cell **A12** should read: "**Cost of Using Surface Mail is $99.56**"

In cell A12 enter the following formula:

="Cost of Using " & INDEX(A7:C9, MATCH ($B$2,$B$7:$B$9,0),1) & " is " & DOLLAR(VLOOKUP(B2,B7:C9,2,FALSE))

Ex4_Q3.

On the **Chart** worksheet, create an **Exponential Trendline** based on the **YR2010** data series. Include a future trend of 2.5.

1. Click the chart.
2. Click the **Chart Element** icon that appears to the right of the chart
3. From the list of chart elements click the arrow to the right of "**Trendline**"
4. Click "**More Options**"
5. On the **Add a Trendline based on Series:** dialog box, select **YR2010** and click **OK**
6. On the "**Format Trendline**" task pane, click "**Trendline Options**"
7. Select the "**Exponential**" option

8. In the "**Forecas**t" section, enter 2.5 in the "**Forward**" textbox
9. Close the task pane

Ex4_Q4.

In the **Consolidation** worksheet, in cell **A2,** consolidate the Expenses data in the "**Office Records**" sheet using the following ranges: **A10:B23**; **E10:F23**; **A30:B43**; **E30:F43**; **A50:B63**; **E50:F63** and **A70:B83**. Use the **SUM** function for the consolidation and add labels from the left column.

1. Select cell **A2** in the **Consolidation** worksheet.
2. Click **Data** ⇨ **Data Tools** ⇨ **Consolidate. Ensure that the cursor is in the "Reference" textbox.**
3. On the **Office Records** worksheet, select range **A10:B23**
4. Click **Add** in the consolidate dialog box
5. Repeat steps **3** and **4** for **E10:F23**; **A30:B43**; **E30:F43**; **A50:B63**; **E50:F63** and **A70:B83**
6. In the **Consolidate** dialog box, in the "**Use label in**" section, select the "**Left column**" checkbox.
7. On the **Consolidate** dialog box click **OK.**

Ex4_Q5.

The **Choose Function** worksheet has 3 option buttons for mailing types and costs. Cell **B2** is a linked cell for the option buttons. Using the data in cells **A7:C9** and the linked cell, use the CHOOSE function to construct a formula that will display the following information in cell **A12**:

a. When you select **Option 1** (**Air Mail**), cell **A12** should read: "**Cost of Using Air Mail is $124.78**"
b. When you select **Option 2** (**Courier**), cell **A12** should read: "**Cost of Using Courier is $450**"
c. When you select **Option 3** (**Surface Mail**) cell **A12** should read: "**Cost of Using Surface Mail is $99.56**"

In cell **A12** type the following formula:

="The Cost of Using " & CHOOSE (B2, A7, A8, A9) & " is " & DOLLAR (CHOOSE (B2, C7, C8, C9))

Hint:
Use the CHOOSE function twice.

Ex4_Q6

In the **Advanced Filter** worksheet, use range **A3:G4** as the **Criteria Range** to filter the data (**A5:G21**). The filtered data should display:

a. **Advanced Computers** accounts with overdue invoices (**Days Overdue > 0**) AND
b. **Pure Software** accounts with overdue invoices > $2,000
The filtered information should be similar to the following:

Figure Ex4_Q6

1. In cell **A3** enter "**Pure Software**"
2. In cell **A4** enter "**Advanced Computers**"
3. In cell **D3** enter "**>2000**"
4. In cell **G3** enter "**>0**"
5. In cell **G4** enter "**>0**"
6. Click **Data** ⇨ **Sort & Filter** ⇨ **Advanced**
7. On the **Advanced Filter** dialog box:
   a. In the **List Range** text box, select range **A5:G21**
   b. In the **Criteria Range** text box, select range **A2:G4** and click **OK**

Ex4_Q7.

In the **Database Function** worksheet, range **A7:G22** is a table (database) named "**Invoice**". Using range **A2:A3** as **Criteria Range,** with **A3** as the criteria cell, in cell G3 compute the average invoice amount for the "**Pure Software**" account. Use the **DAVERAGE** function and table a table specifier.

1. In cell **A2** enter "**Account Name**"
2. In cell **A3** enter "**Pure Software**"
3. In cell **G3** enter the following formula:
=DAVERAGE(Invoice[#All],"Invoice Amount", A2:A3)

Ex4_Q8.

Using the Pivot Table worksheet, create the Pivot Table shown below:

Figure Ex4_Q8

1. **Click any cell within the data**
2. **Click Insert** ⇨ **PivotTable**
3. **In the Create PivotTable dialog box, choose the "Select a table or range option"**
4. **In the "Table/Range" textbox enter (or highlight) the data source (A1:E651)**
5. **Select the "New Worksheet" option for the location of the PivotTable and click OK.**
6. **In the PivotTable Fields task pane, drag the fields into the areas as follows:**

   a. **Column: Province field**
   b. **Row: Salesperson fields**
   c. **Value: Amount field**
   d. **Filter: Order Date**

Ex4_Q9.

Use the **PivotTable** worksheet to compute the relative importance of each promotional method with respect to the items on promotion.

1. Right-click any cell inside the data field
2. Select "**Summarize Values By:**" and click the **SUM** calculation
3. Right-click any cell inside the data field
4. Select **Show Values As**, Index.

Note: The higher the index value, the more important the cell is in the overall results.

Ex4_Q10.

The **Calculated Column** worksheet contains a Pivot Table. Create a calculated column in the Pivot Table called "**Difference**" that computes the difference between the monthly **Actual** and **Projected** values (**Actual – Projected**).

1. Click any cell in the Pivot Table data area
2. Select **Analyze** ⇨ **Calculation**s ⇨ **Fields, Items, & Sets** drop-down
3. In the Name text box enter "**Difference**"
4. In the Formula text box enter "**=Actual – Projected**"
5. Click Add. Click **OK**

Ex4_Q11.

On the **Product Margin** worksheet, use the appropriate **What-If Analysis** tool and the data on the sheet to determine at what price an item must be sold (**Unit Price**) to obtain a **Margin** of **30 percent**.

Note: Enter 30 percent as 0.3

1. Click **Data** ⇨ **Data Tools** ⇨ **What-If Analysis**
2. On the Drop-down, select **Goal Seek**…and enter the information as shown in the figure below
Figure Ex4_Q11

You should obtain a margin of 29.93% at a unit price of appro. $37.18.

Ex4_Q12.

In the "**Computers**" worksheet, in cell **F14**, write a formula to compute the sum of the total cost for **Division 3** computers. Utilize the existing "**Computers**" range name (called "**Parts**") in your formula.

In cell F14, enter the following formula:

=SUMIF(Computers[Division], "=3", Computers[Total Cost])

Ex4_Q13.

In the **PureTraining** folder in your **Documents** folder, there is a workbook called "**Copysheet.xlxs**. Copy the worksheet called "**CopyMe**" into the current workbook. Place it before "**Sheet1**"

1. In the current workbook, click **File** ➪ **Open**
2. Open the **Copysheet.xlxs** in your **PureTraining** folder
3. Right-click "**CopyMe**" worksheet tab and select "**Move or Copy**"
4. In the **To book**: dropdown, select **Ex4_Q14** workbook.
5. In the Before sheet list, select "**Sheet1**"
6. Tick the **Create a copy** checkbox and click **OK**

Ex4_Q14.

In the **Customer Contact Details** sheet, configure print options to print column headers (row 6) on every printout page.

1. Choose **Page Layout** ➪ **Page Setup** ➪ **Print Titles**.
2. Activate the "**In the Rows to repeat at top**:" text box in the **Sheet** tab, .
3. Highlight row 6 (the header row) and click **OK**.

Ex4_Q15.

Format the "**Headers & Footers**" worksheet so that on the printout, page headers will be printed as follows:

Left section: Current Date

Middle section: "Pure Software Training"

Right section: Page x of y

1. Click **View** ➪ **Workbook Views** ➪ **Page Layout.**
2. On the **Page Layout** view of the worksheet, activate the page header by clicking at the top.
3. In the left box of the page header, enter **&[Date].**
4. In the centre box of the page header, enter "**Pure Software Training && Consulting**".
5. In the right box of the page header, enter **Page &[Page] of &[Pages].**
6. Click anywhere on the sheet outside of the page header.

Ex4_Q16.

On the "**Headers & Footers**" sheet, apply the following **Page Setup** settings:

Bottom margin **= 0**; Page Centre= **Horizontally & Vertically**;

Page Orientation = **Landscape**; Paper Size = **B5**.

Copy these settings to the **FormatMe1** and **FormatMe2** sheets

1. **Activate the "Header & Footer" sheet**
2. **Click Page Layout tab.**
3. **On the Page Setup group, click the dialog launcher** ⬓
4. **On the Page Setup window, select the Page tab and select the Landscape option for Orientation.**
5. **In the Paper Size text box select B5 from the dropdown**
6. **Select the Margins tab and enter 0 in the Spin Button for the Buttom margin.**
7. **In the Centre on page section, select both the horizontal and vertical boxes and click OK.**
8. **Select the "Headers and Footers" sheet. While pressing the Ctlr Key, activate both the FormatMe1 and FormatMe2 sheets. This will select all three sheets as a group.**
9. **With the three sheets selected, click the Page Setup dialog launcher.**
10. **When the Page Setup window opens, close it again. This will transfer the settings for the source sheet ("Headers & Footers") to the other two sheets.**
11. **Right-click one of the three sheets and click "Ungroup Sheets" in the context menu.**

Ex4_Q17.

Provide the appropriate settings on the "**Chart**" sheet so that when the sheet is printed only the data will be printed. The chart should <u>not</u> be printed along with the data.

1. Right-click the <u>chart area</u> and select "**Format Chart Area**" from the context menu.
2. In the **Format Chart Area** dialog screen, click the "**Size & Properties**" icon
3. Click the arrow that points to "**Properties**" to expand it.
4. Uncheck the "**Print Object**" checkbox

Ex4_Q18.

Using the Custom Views worksheet as parent sheet, create a custom view with column C and column D hidden. Leave all other columns unhidden. Name the custom view "My Custom View".

1. **In the Custom View sheet, highlight columns C and D.**
2. **Right-click on the highlighted range and select "Hide" from the context menu.**
3. **Click View ⇨ Workbook Views ⇨ Custom Views.**
4. **On the Custom View screen, click the Add button.**
5. **In the Add View screen, enter "My Custom View" in the Name textbox.**

Ex4_Q19.

You work for a company called "**ThreePointEight Consulting**". Configure Excel options such that when you type "**3Pt8**" into a cell, the cell should display your company's name (i.e. "**ThreePointEight Consulting**")

1. **Select File ⇨ Options ⇨ Proofing**
2. **Click the "AutoCorrect Options…" button**
3. **In the "Replace:" textbox, type "3Pt8"**
4. **In the "With:" textbox, type "ThreePointEight Consulting"**
5. **Click OK**

Ex4_Q21.

Provide the required print options so that Excel will print the 2 comments on the "**Printing**" sheet at the end of the printout.

1. **Click Page Layout on the Ribbon.**
2. **Click the Page Setup dialog launcher**
3. **Select the Sheet tab**
4. **In the Comments dropdown, select "At the end of sheet" and click OK**

Ex4_Q22.

On the **Pivot Table** sheet, add a second instance of the **Location** field to the **Value** section. Change the name of that value to "**Pct**". Show each value of the **Pct** field as percent of the total of the (**Pct**) column.

1. Click a cell within the pivot table data so show the **Pivot Table Fields task pane**.
2. Drag the **Location** field to the **Value** section.
3. Click on the field (just added the **Value** section) and select "**Value Field Settings…**"
4. In the **Custom Name** box, type "**Pct**" and click **OK**
5. Right-click any cell under the **Pct** column and select **Show value As % of Column Total.**

Ex4_Q23.

9. CHANGE THIS QUESTION… SEE SHEET

Notes:

2. If the formula that is entered into the conditional formatting dialog box contains a cell reference, that reference is considered a *relative reference*, based on the upper-left cell in the selected range.

Ex4_Q24.

On the Budget – Division 1 worksheet, paste the list of range names starting from cell I5.

1. Select cell I5
2. Select Formula, Use in Formula, Paste Names (or Press F3)
3. Click Paste List.

Notes:

1. In cell **A1** enter: **=Today()**
2. Click the dialog box launcher of the **Home ⇨ Font** tab
3. Click the **Number** tab. In the **Category** list select the **Custom** option
4. In the **Type** box enter the following format: **[RED]mmmm dd, yyyy (dddd)**

** ** Open the Custom Format Example sheet to see examples of custom formatting.**

Ex4_Q25.

Apply the **General** format as the <u>default</u> format for the workbook.

Notes:

1. Select the **Home** tab ⇨ **Style** ⇨ **Cell Style** drop-down.
2. Right-click the **Normal** style ⇨ **Modify**. Select the **General** format. Click **OK**.

Ex4_Q26.

On the **West Companies** sheet, modify the existing **Conditional Formatting** rule to remove the values from then **2015 Sales** column and show only the data bars.

Notes:

1. Click **Home** ⇨ **Styles** ⇨ **Conditional Formatting** ⇨ **Manage Rules**
2. On the **Show format rule for** drop-down box select "**This Worksheet**"
3. Activate the **Data Bar** rule and click **Edit Rule…**
4. Click the **Show bar only** text box

='Jan Humidity'!B2>B2

Ex4_Q27.

On the **Feb Humidity** sheet, highlight (using Red colour) all humidity values that are **less** than their corresponding **Jan Humidity** values.

Notes:

1. Select the humidity values on the **Feb Humidity** sheet (**B2:H21**).
2. Click **Home** ⇨ **Styles** ⇨ **Conditional Formatting** drop-down
3. Select the **Manage Rules…** option
4. On the **Conditional Formatting Rules Manager** dialog box, click the **New Rule** tab.
5. Select the **Use a formula to determine which cells to format** option.
6. In the **Format values where this formula is true** text box, type the following formula: '**Jan Humidity**'!B2>B2
7. Click the **Format** tab and in the **Colour** drop-down select **Red.**

Ex4_Q28.

In the **Auto Fill** sheet, Create an **Auto Fill** using the cities in cells **A3:A11**. Type **Sydney** in cell **C3** and drag the **Fill handler** to auto-fill cells **C4:C11** with the rest of the cities (just as in cells **A3:A11**).

Notes:

1. Click **File** ⇨ **Options** ⇨ **Advanced**.
2. Scroll down and click the **Edit Custom List** button.
3. In the **List entries** list box enter the cities (**Sydney……..Newcastle**)
4. Click **Add** and then click **OK**
5. In the **Auto Fill** sheet, select cell **C3**, enter **Sydney**
6. Drag down to fill the cells

Ex4_Q29.

In the Status Chart worksheet, change the chart layout to Layout 1, change the chart title to Employment History and change the chart style to Style 9. Save the chart as a chart template to the PureSoftwareTemplate folder in your documents folder and with the name EmploymentChart

Notes:

1. Select the Status Chart worksheet. On this worksheet, select the chart
2. Click Chart Tools Design Chart Layouts group and click the Quick Layout dropdown, and select Layout 1
3. Click on Chart Title and type "Employment History"
4. In the Chart Tools Design tab, locate the Chart Styles group and click the drop down. Select Style 9
5. Right click the chart and click Save as Template. Navigate to the PureSoftwareTemplate folder in your documents folder, name the template EmploymentChart and click Save.

Ex4_Q30.

Using a named formula called "**Address**", the **INDEX** function and the **MATCH** function, provide a means to retrieve the address into cell **G3** for a name entered in cell **G1**. Use one of the names in the **A3:A10** range. Ensure that no error message is shown if the name does not exist in the list. If the name does not exist the address cell (**G3**) must be blank.

Notes:

1. Click **Formula** ⇨ **Define Names** ⇨ **Define Name**
2. In the **New Name** dialog box, enter "**Address**" into the **Name** textbox
3. In the "**Refers to:**" textbox, enter:
   =IFERROR (INDEX($A$3:$B$10, MATCH($G$1,$A$3:$A$10,0),2),"") and click **OK**